YOUR INNER
SUPERPOWER

EVERYTHING YOU NEED
IS WITHIN YOU ALL
ALONG

Anderson Brown

Table of Contents

PART 1

Chapter 1:

How to Embrace Adventure to Change Your Life

Human beings are creatures of habit. This can be a good thing, as the habits we form can allow us to autopilot through the more tedious aspects of life. But as the years go by, many of us put not only a few habits but our *entire lives* on autopilot. And when we do so, we develop a problem of *sameness*. We stagnate, and our once-steady supply of new experiences dries up.

So what's the cost of this?

When we stop engaging in the new, we stop developing as people. We stop growing. And when we stop growing, the monotony and boredom set in, often felt in the form of a nagging feeling that something just isn't right in our lives. If that sounds like you, it might be time to break out of the habits causing you to stagnate. To help you do this, let's look at ways you can bring adventure back into your life.

You get up. You eat a lackluster breakfast. You rush to work. You get off at 6. You watch television for a few hours. You go to bed. You repeat. Sound familiar?

Sameness has a way of making us feel like monotony is normal. We stop living, begin merely existing, and—amazingly—we feel comfortable in that. But the simple act of shaking up your routine can open your eyes to the world of adventure that's always just outside your door.

Add a Third Space

What's a third place, you might ask? In short, it's one of the keys to adventure!

A third place is somewhere that is separate from your two most-visited social environments: work and home. It's the local coffee shop where you might go to work on your latest short story. It's the barbershop where you'd go to have a chat about the latest happenings in the neighborhood. It's the library you run for when you need a quiet moment of contemplation.

Unlike someone's first place, which is the home, and the second place, which is work, the third place tends to blend community life and self-expression. It's a place where, unlike at work, you can relax and be yourself, and unlike at home, you're pushed to explore new possibilities, often through social interaction. Finding your third place, whatever that might be, is essential to breaking up the monotony of life and finding new adventures and new people. Start scouring your neighborhood for one today!

Choose a New Path

It's the experience of life that we remember the most, and it is the memories of these experiences make us happiest in old age. Regret is built upon a life of sameness—don't let that be you.

Change your habits. Change your life. Find adventure.

Now, get out there and do it.

Chapter 2:

How To Achieve Peak Performance In Your Career

What exactly do we mean by peak performance? Well, it is defined as the state when you are at your best, delivering the results and feeling in the flow. You're able to overcome the challenges and feel at ease about your work and life. Getting in a state of peak performance at work is all about being motivated, managing your energy, staying productive, and developing the proper habits. We have a finite supply of energy that we expend throughout the day, but we aren't taught how to cultivate this energy. The ultimate key to higher performance is learning how to manage your energy all through the day consciously. The challenge is, once you have reached your peak performance, you have to stay and perform in that state as constantly as possible; you have to sustain the level of peak performance. Here are some ways for you to achieve peak performance in your career.

1. Being Motivated About The Work

The best way to stay motivated I to choose something that you're both good at and love to do. Work on something that keeps you energized and motivated. When you do this type of work, you're more likely to operate in a flow state and achieve peak performance. But, as much as we like, there won't always be things that favor our interest. In those situations, it's helpful to reframe the problem that fits the "why" purpose. For example, if you are unwilling to do something, but there's an urgency, and you're bound to do it, you will find a way and energy to get with it anyway. It would be best to start focusing on the gains and benefits you will get from doing the things you dislike. This will keep you somewhat motivated to do it. Or you can ask for help from someone who loves doing the work that you hate. It's all about reframing the situations to your best interest.

2.   Developing The Right Habits

Achieving peak performance is more about the actions you take and the thoughts you think. Having negative thoughts like "will I be able to do it?" or "what if he/she is better at it than me?" and so forth will only make you anxious. It will be like driving with the handbrake on, and your performance will only be a drag. Instead, try and develop positive thoughts. Get on with the attitude of "I can do it" or "I can learn from my colleagues if I mess up." Adopting such positive thoughts will give you a huge boost towards your peak performance. Behavior habits can also hurt your performance just as severely. For example, if you have a habit of arriving late, start getting ready 10-20 minutes earlier than you usually do. If you are afraid to speak up, try saying anything for the first 60 seconds, so your voice is at least heard.

3.   Staying Productive

Alongside having the motivation and the right habits, try to get more work done with the same or fewer resources; whether it's time, money, energy, you'll be steps ahead. Being productive also means that you can create extra time for the next task, thinking, or simply to recharge. Banishing obstacles like procrastination and perfectionism can help you achieve your peak performance. Address the things that are holding you back. Assess and evaluate them, stay on track by planning your day the night before.

4. Managing Your Energy

You can generate more and more of your energy, that's the best thing about it. It is a renewable resource, while time is not. Therefore, it is essential to manage your energy and protect your time. One way you can manage your energy is by matching your tasks with the day that best suits you. If you are more productive and creative in the morning, start doing the more significant and more critical tasks in that time, and leave the small ones for later. The prominent energy creators revolve around your health and wellness, both physical and mental. Get a good night's sleep every day, have a proper diet, and exercise regularly.

5. Be Consistent

The single most important thing you can do for your career is to show up every day. No skill or talent can beat the power of consistency. Being consistent will continue to maximize your potential for peak performance and give you an upper hand over those who tend to take the opposite of consistency. As you continue to learn and apply the new lessons you have learned from your experience at work, your ability to perform at peak will stay on the upward side of the scale longer than expected.

Conclusion

Above everything else, we should remember that sustaining peak performance at work doesn't have to be your hit or miss gamble. You should know your numbers and plot out strategies for compounding improvements and set measurable goals to work. This will give you not only a progressive routine but also some direction and clarity. Embrace the momentum tum to stay in the flow state longer than your co-workers or the last time you did. Track your performance and continue to beat your current record to keep yourself motivated and full of confidence.

Chapter 3:

9 Habits To Wake Up Early

Waking up early is a real struggle for many people. People are battling this friendly monster silently. Friendly because the temptation to snooze the alarm or turn it off completely when it rings in the morning is irresistible. Almost everyone can attest to cursing under their breath when they hear their alarm go off loudly in the morning.

Here are 9 habits that you should strive to incorporate into your life if you wish to make waking early a part of your routine:

1. Sleeping early.

It is simple – early to bed, early to rise. Retiring to bed early will give you enough time to exhaust your sleep. The average person ought to have at least 8 hours of sleep. Sleeping early will create more time for rest and enable you to wake up on time.

Since sleep is not ignorable, you may be embarrassed when you find yourself sleeping when attending a meeting, or when you are at work. Save yourself this shame by sleeping early to wake up earlier.

After a long day of vicissitudes, gift your body the pleasure of having a good night's rest. Create extra time for this by lying horizontally early enough.

2. Scheduling your plans for the day beforehand.

A good plan is a job half done. Before the day ends, plan for the activities of the next day. When it is all mapped out, you will sleep with a clear mind on what you will be facing the next day. Planning is not a managerial routine task alone but everyone's duty of preparing to fight the unknown the following day.

Waking up early is a difficult decision to make impromptu because of the weakness in yielding to the temptation of 'sleeping for only five more minutes.' Having a plan gives you a reason to wake up early.

3. Creating deadlines.

Working under pressure is an alternative motivation for waking up early if planning has failed. With assignments to submit within a short time, or work reports to be submitted on short notice, the need to wake up early to beat these deadlines will be automatic.

We can create deadlines and ultimatums for ourselves without waiting on our superiors to impose them on us. This self-drive will last longer and it will increase our productivity instead of waiting for our clients and employers to give us ultimatums.

4. Being psychologically prepared.

The mind is the powerhouse of the body. Mental preparedness is the first step towards making and sticking to landmark decisions. The mind should initiate and accept the idea of waking up early before you can comfortably adopt this new routine.

Develop a positive attitude towards rising early and all other subsequent results will fall in place. The first person you need to convince to move towards a particular cause is you. As simple as waking up early seems, many people are grappling with late coming.

This is fixable by making a conscious decision to turn around your sleeping habits. The greatest battle is fought in the mind, where the body antagonizes the spirit.

5. <u>Finding like-minded friends.</u>

Birds of the same feathers flock together. When you are in the company of friends with one routine, your habits are fortified. With no dissenting voice amongst your friends to discourage you from waking up early, your morning routine will find a permanent spot in your life.

The contrary is true. When you are the odd one out in a clique of friends who have no regard for time, you are likely to lose even the little time-consciousness you had. They will contaminate you with their habits and before you know it, you will slip back to your old self (an over sleeper).

When you also decide to be a loner and not associate with those with the same habits as yourself, then you risk giving up on the way. The psych from friends will be lacking and soon you will just revert to your old habits.

When you want to walk fast, walk alone. When you want to go far, walk with others.

6. <u>Being sensitive to your environment.</u>

It takes a man of understanding to read and understand the prevailing times and seasons. You may occasionally visit a friend or a relative and spend the night. How can you wake up way past sunrise in a foreign environment? This will suggest to your hosts that you are lazy.

Create a good image by waking up a little bit early. If allowed, help do some morning chores over there.

Adjust your routine accordingly. Win over people by waking up early to join them in their morning chores. It is there where friendships are forged. A simple habit of waking up early can be an avenue to make alliances.

7. Addressing any health issues early.

In case of any underlying health conditions that can stop you from waking up early in the morning, seek medical help fast. You may be willing to be an early riser but may be suffering from asthma triggered by the chilly weather in the morning.

When that condition is controlled, you can also manage to wake up a little bit earlier than before and engage in health-friendly activities in the morning. It is a win-win. In either case, going for a medical check-up frequently will keep you healthy to wake up early.

Your health is a priority and when taken care of you will wake up early.

8. It is a habit for the successful.

Ironically, those who have made it in life wake up earlier than the less established ones. One would think that it is the place of the less-founded ones to rise early to go to work and do business so that they can be at par with the wealthy and mighty. Instead, the reverse is true.

Follow the footsteps of great leaders who wake up early to attend to their affairs. They have become who they are because they give no room to the laziness of waking up late. We all have 24 hours in a day to do our businesses, where does the gap between the haves and the have-nots come from? That gap comes from how we use our time.

9. Having a cheerful Spirit.

A cheerful spirit finds joy in even what seems trivial. You should not see waking up early as punishment. It should be a routine to be followed happily religiously. When you have a cheerful spirit, knowing for whose benefit you rise early, then it will be a habit engraved into your spirit.

The above 9 habits to wake up early are key to discovering our purpose and build a new routine henceforth of being an early riser. The most successful people in the world abide by this routine so why not make it yours too.

Chapter 4:

10 Habits of Bernard Arnault

Bernard Arnault- French investor, businessman, and CEO of LVMH recently reclaimed the title "worlds' wealthiest" from fellow billionaire Jeff Bezos. His business acumen and awe-inspiring financial achievements deserve to be recognized. His perspective can serve as a model for entrepreneurs who want to follow in his footsteps.

Bernard Arnault has written about money, prosperity, leadership, and power over the years. Moreover, his path to becoming the CEO of one of the world's most recognized brands will provide you with valuable lessons to emulate from. That is, your life circumstances shouldn't stop you from expanding and thriving outside your expertise.

Following his impressive accomplishments, here are ten points you can take away from Arnault's journey to success.

1. Happiness Before Money

According to Bernard, happiness is leading. That is leading your team to the top whether you are in business, sports, music industry. Money, according to him, is a consequence, and success is a blend of your past and future.

Your priority is not what you'll make sooner! When you put much-required effort into your job, profits will flow.

2. Mistakes Your Lesson

Your biggest mistake is your learning opportunity. When your business isn't performing well, understand the situation first and be patient.

In the world of innovative brands, it can take years to get something to work. Give it time and put yourself in a long-term expectation.

3. Always Behave as a Startup

Think small. Act quickly. Smaller boats can turn faster than more giant tankers. Arnault emphasizes the significance of thinking small. LVMH, in Arnault's opinion, is not a massive corporation device with miles of unnecessary bureaucracy.

Believe in your vision while attracting the best talent for your success path. A handy, adaptable speed, one that can fail quickly as easy to sleeve up.

4. Continuously Reinvent Yourself

How do you maintain your relevance? Bernard's LVMH is built on innovation, quality, entrepreneurship, and, essentially, on long-term vision. LVMH excels at developing increasingly desirable new products and selling them globally.

To be successful today, with your capabilities, opt for a worldwide startup and see what's going on. This necessitates a more considerable investment, which gives you an advantage. However, let the Creators run your inventions.

5. Team-Creative Control

Arnault strategies find creative control under each product's team to do what they do best. Arnault's designers are the dreamer's realists and critics. Allow your team to take creative control. You risk putting a tourniquet around their minds if you restrict them in any way.

6. Create Value To Attract Customers

Marketing investigates what the customer desires. As a result, you are doing what they need: creating a product and testing it to see if it works. Keeping your products in close contact with consumers, according to Arnault, makes a desire to buy in them. LVMH creates products that generate customers. For him, it's never about sales; it's always about creating desire. Your goal should be to be desirable for long-term marketability.

7. Trust the Process

There will always be different voices in business, and while there will undoubtedly be good advice, if you believe an idea will succeed, you may need to persevere until the end. Like Arnault, disregard your critics by following through with your vision to excel.

8. Your Persistence Is Everything

It would be best if you were very persistent. It would be best to have ideas, but the idea is only 20% of the equation. The execution rate is 80%. So if you are trying out a startup, having ideas marvellous, the driving force is persistence and execution.

When it comes to the most successful startups, such as Facebook, the idea was great from the beginning. Others, however, had the same idea. So why is Facebook such a phenomenal success today? It is critically through execution with persistence.

9. Do Not Think of Yourself

Bernard Arnault can be differentiated from other billionaires like Elon Musk or Bill Gates by focusing on the brands, making their longevity rather than making himself the face. He is only concerned with promoting his products.

To accomplish this, you must maintain contact with pioneers and designers, for example, while also making their ideas more specific and sustainable.

10. Maintain Contact With Your Company

One of the most common leadership mistakes is to lose sight of the company once you reach the top and "stick" with manageable goals. Instead, to see if the machine is working correctly or if there is room for improvement, you must examine every corner and every part of it.

Conclusion

Your willingness to outwork and your ability to outlearn everyone will keep your success journey intact and going. Bernard Arnault's path to becoming the CEO of the worlds most recognized and desired multibillion empire of brands have a valuable lesson for you: your starting point does not influence or determine your future destination.

Chapter 5:

How Getting Out of Your Comfort Zone Could Be The Best Thing Ever

A comfort zone is best described as the place where you feel comfortable and your abilities are not being tested, or a place where you don't have to try anything new or different. We have all heard the advice of getting out of our comfort zone. Its sure sounds like an easy phrase, but any advice is easier to give than to take. While it is true that the ability to take risks by stepping outside your comfort zone is the primary way by which we grow, it's also true that we are often afraid to take that first step. Embracing new experiences can bloom your life and could even change the direction of your career. Comfort zones are not really about comfort; and they are about fear. So, break the chains and step out; you will enjoy the process of taking risks and growing. Here are some ways to get out of your comfort zone to experience a better life.

1. Become Aware Of What's Outside The Comfort Zone

You believe so many things are worth doing, but the thought of disappointment and failure always holds you back. Identify the things that you are afraid of doing and assess the discomforts associated with them. Start working on them slowly and gradually. You will see how much progress you will make and how much you will grow following that. Once your discomforts no longer scare you, you will see how confident you will become in trying new things.

2. Have A Clear Sight About What You Have To Overcome

There would be many situations that get you anxious and uncomfortable. Please make a list of all of them and go deeper. The primary emotion associated with all of our negative thoughts that we try to overcome is fear. Are you afraid of public speaking because you are insecure about your voice? Do you get nervous around people and avoid talking to them for fear of being ignored? Be specific in your areas of discomfort, and then work on your insecurities to get more confident.

3. Get Comfortable With Discomfort

Expand your comfort zone to get out of it. Make it your goal to stop running away from the discomforts. If you can't make eye contact while talking, try locking it a bit more rather than immediately looking out. If you stay long enough and practice it, it will start to become less uncomfortable.

4. See Failure As A Teacher

Many of us are so scared of failures that we would prioritize doing absolutely nothing other than taking a shot at our dreams and goals. We have to treat our failures as a teacher. We learn more from failures than we do from successes. Take that experience that has caused you to fail and evaluate how you can take that lesson your next time so that the chance of success increases. Many of the world's famous people, and even billionaires and millionaires, failed the thousandth time before succeeding.

5. Take Baby Steps

Don't try to achieve everything at once. If you jump outside your comfort zone, the chances are that you will become overwhelmed and jump right back in. Always start by taking small steps, overcome the fear of little things first. It's the small steps along the journey that ensures our extraordinary destination. If you are afraid of public speaking, start by speaking to a smaller group of people or even your family and friends. This will help you built self-confidence, and you will be ready to talk on public platforms in no time.

6. Hang out with risk-takers:

If you want to become better at something, start hanging out with people who already took the risk, who already are doing the things you planned to do. Start emulating them. No one can give you the best insight into the situations than those who already have experienced it. Almost inevitably, their influence will start affecting your behavior, and you too will get a clear mind about things.

7. Be Honest With Yourself

Stop making excuses for the things that you are too afraid to do. You might be tricking your brain into thinking that maybe you don't have enough time to do your tasks. But in reality, you are scared of giving it a chance and risking failure. Don't make excuses but instead, be honest. You will be in a better place to confront what is truly bothering you, and this will increase your chance of moving forward.

8. Identify New Opportunities

Staying in your comfort zone is like sitting in a closed room or wearing blinders. You will convince yourself that you already dislike the things you didn't even try yet and only care about the already part of your life. But you have to put your walls down, not thickens them, and take risks. You will be amazed at how many opportunities you will be exposed to when you finally let yourself out.

Conclusion

It will seem scary at first to get out of your comfort zone, but it will be the best experience of your life. Don't jump right out of it; slowly push yourself past your comfort zone. You will eventually feel more and more comfortable about the new stuff you were too afraid to try.

Chapter 6:

10 Habits For A Clean Home

A clean home can make the homeowner a lot happier, less stressed, and even calmer. Waking up or coming back to a clutter-free and organized home can instantly brighten our mornings or even lift up our moods. But the thought of having to clean it extensively on weekends, for long hours, only to find the space in an absolute mess by midweek is like a nightmare and crestfallen.

Trust me when I say it is not that difficult maintaining a clean home. You need not necessarily have to deep clean your house almost every weekend for hours if you incorporate few very habits in your everyday routines. Today, we are exactly going to talk on this topic and hope to enlighten you to create a clean space.

Here are ten habits for a clean and happy home:

1. Make Your Bed As Soon as You Wake Up

We have heard a million times that the first thing that we should do after waking up is to make our beds, but how many of us incorporate this habit daily? An unmade bed can pull down the overall appearance of your bedroom by making it look messy. So take few moments and tuck those sheets and put your pillows in order. Change your bed sheets or duvet covers, and pillow covers as and when necessary.

Making our beds clean our most comfortable and visible area in the house and gives a sense of achievement helps us stay motivated and in a fresh state of mind throughout the day. If tucking in bed sheets daily is too annoying for you simply switch to duvet covers; that might save you from some hassle.

2. Put Things Back in Place After Using Them

Almost every home has this one chair or one spot that is cluttered with clothes and random knick-knacks, and this area hardly gets cleaned. Moreover, it is a normal human tendency to go on to dump more and more pieces of stuff and increase the pile size.

The idea behind creating this pile is that you will put away all the things in one go in a single day, but who are we kidding? As the pile starts increasing, we start pushing away the task of keeping the things back in their original place. The best way to avoid creating clutter is to put things back in their true place as soon as their job is done.

I completely understand that after finishing a task, we never feel like getting up to put them back in their home and hinder the task until we feel like doing so. But if you can consciously put this little effort into not letting things sit on the ground or in random places and put them back as soon as their job is done for the day, it is going to save a lot of time and help you have a clean space.

This is also applicable to your freshly washed clothes. As soon as you have them cleaned, fold them and put them in the drawer where it belongs. This will save you the headache of doing so on a Saturday morning which can then be used for reading your favorite book.

3. Take Your Mess With You as You Leave the Room

This is another essential practice that can bring a huge difference in your life and your home if turned into a habit. The idea here is to try not to leave a room empty-handed. What does this mean?

Let us take an example to understand this. Suppose you are in your living room and are going to the kitchen to drink water. Before you leave the living room, scan the room and look if any dirty bowl or plate is sitting in the room that needs to go to the kitchen. Take that cutlery along with you and keep them in the sink or dishwasher.

After making this a habit, you can then start following the one-touch rule that states that you touch a used item only once! That means if you are taking out the trash, make sure to dump or dispose of it properly and not just take it out and keep it somewhere on the porch or garden as this will kill the whole idea behind the habit. If you are moving something, it is better that you keep them where they belong, else, leave them be.

4.   Have a House Cleaning Schedule

Maintain cleaning schedules like morning cleaning routines or weekly cleaning routines. This is basically distributing the cleaning of the entire house over an entire week rather than keeping the task to get done in a single day. Fix days for achieving a particular task, like on Wednesdays you can vacuum the living room and the bedroom and on Thursdays clean the other rooms and so on.

Make sure to assign 15 to 20 minutes each morning that you will strictly use for cleaning purposes. This will surely bring about a very positive impact on your house, and you will be in awe of how much cleaning can be done in those mere 15 - 20 minutes. Try to vacuum the hallways, entries, and all other high traffic regions of your home (including the kitchen) as frequently as possible as they tend to get dusty easily.

5.   Maintain a Laundry Routine

Maintain a proper laundry routine depending on whether you live alone or in a family. As the pile of clothes grows enough to go into the washing, do the needful immediately. Do not delay the task endlessly as remember it is always easier to wash one load of clothing at a day rather than washing multiple loads of cloth in a day.

If you live with a family, do laundry every alternate day and if you live alone, then make sure to do your laundry every weekend. Also, make it a habit of putting the dirty clothes in the basket immediately after changing out of it rather than keeping them at random places to wash them later.

6. Keep Your Shoes, Coats, and Umbrellas in Their Right Place

Make it a habit to open your shoes near the entrance, put them away properly, and not randomly throw them. Keep a basket near the entryway where you can store all the umbrellas. If possible, put up a key holder on the door to keep the car keys and door keys in an organized manner.

The same goes for your long coats. Do not just dump them anywhere right after returning home! Have hooks hidden behind the entry door or have a sleek cupboard near the exit to store the trenchcoats and the long coats away from sight. These little changes will instantly clean up space.

7. Relax Only After Finishing Your Chores

If you have a chore that requires immediate attention, do it! Do not sit and relax, as this will go on to delay the chore indefinitely, and you may even forget to do it. So get your chores done first, then sit and watch Netflix. Detain your tasks only when you are exhausted and desperately need a break.

8. Clean After Every Meal

Right after fishing your meal, clean up the place. I know what most of you are thinking, but trust me, relaxing after cleaning everything up will give you more satisfaction and help you have a cleaner home for sure. After having your lunch or dinner, keep all the plates in the washer and make sure to also clean the utensils that you used for cooking.

Clean the countertops, the burners, and also the table that you sat and ate on. Cleaning the countertops and tables immediately will save your furniture from an ugly stain and help you save a lot of energy and time you might have had to put in if you try to clean the spill the later day.

9. Clean Your Dishes and Sink Every Night

I wanted to say have a nighttime cleaning routine every day where you clean all the dishes from dinner or any other remaining dishes of the day, the sink, and the kitchen by placing all the ingredient containers in their rightful places. The nighttime routine would also include setting your dining table, setting the cushions on your sofa, and clearing out your fridge so that you have a clean and spacious fridge before you unpack your groceries.

But I understand that not many of us have the energy after a hectic day at work, so instead of doing the entire routine, just make sure to wash all the dishes and clean the sink thoroughly so that you wake up to a beautiful kitchen in the morning. I mean, who wants to wake up to a pile of dishes, right? Just give some extra time at night to clean out the kitchen to have a fresh start in the morning.

10. Get Rid Of Unnecessary Things

To have a clutter-free space, each item in your home must have a home of its own. For example, if you do not have a place to hang your towels, they will likely be lying here and there and making the space look messy. Thus, make sure each item has its own place to sleep. If you see there are free-flowing items, then it is time to declutter!

You do not need much space, but you definitely need fewer items that fit in the available space and are easier to manage. More items require more time to clean and put things away properly. Thus, it is easier and requires less time to clean a room with lesser items out on the floor or on the countertop. Hence, make it a habit of getting rid of all the unnecessary items. You can donate the items or gift them to your neighbors or friends. Recycle all the old newspaper and magazines as papers too contribute a lot to the messiness of any room.

Extra Tip: Always try to keep your cleaning supplies in easily visible and accessible areas. This will save you a lot of time and motivate you to clean up anything that should be done as soon as possible.

Be satisfied with clean enough! A home can neither be squeaky clean every day nor can it be cleaned in one day. It is a gradual process that requires a conscious effort being made daily.

A clean home can be easily achieved by following these tips and manifesting these practices as your daily habits.

Chapter 7:

<u>7 Habits To Do Everyday</u>

In the words of Aristotle, *we are what we repeatedly do. Excellence then is not an act, but a habit.* An act that we repeat eventually becomes ingrained in us; it forms part of our culture and lifestyle. We speak, think and act out of the abundance of our hearts.

Here are 7 habits to do every day:

1. <u>Praying</u>

You have heard of the saying that an apple a day keeps the doctor away; but I dare pose to you, a prayer a day keeps the devil away. Praying is not an act for the religious or spiritual. Regardless of your faith, prayer is a pop-up notification in our lives that cannot be put off no matter how often we snooze it.

It has nothing to do with divinity but the humanity in us. Only in prayer can we be vulnerable without fear of it being used against us. We surrender our mortality to the immortal one. Prayer psyches our morale and gives us the confidence to face the uncertainty of tomorrow.

Before talking to mortals, talk to the supernatural in prayer. In solitude, you can only do so much. Prayer provides the much-needed avenue to vent to someone at the other end of the line – God.

2. <u>Reading</u>

Great leaders are readers (read that again). Reading widens our knowledge base and we stay up to date in current affairs. Being among the wisest of his generation, Haile Selassie says *A man who says "I have learned enough and will learn no further" should be considered as knowing nothing at all.*

Knowledge is power. Amass yourself as much of it as possible. Read newspapers and lifestyle magazines to catch up with the fast-moving world, read inspirational and motivational blogs and articles to be inspired to dream bigger, and read business magazines to be at par with innovations that will blow up your mind.

Reading gives you immeasurable exposure. Challenge yourself to read at least two books (even e-books) in one month and watch yourself grow.

3. <u>Cleaning</u>

Cleanliness is next to godliness. It is supposed to be a routine activity, not one to be scheduled to be done on particular days only. There is this misconception, especially in Africa, that cleaning is a gender role. No, it is not. It is everyone's responsibility to keep their immediate environment clean and not delegate it to another person, for there is only so much that they can do.

Most people fail at this because they keep postponing cleaning duties. Why do it later when you can do it now? Do your laundry, wash your utensils, clean your kitchen, take shower, dust off your working space at the office, routinely dust off your laptop or desktop, get a clean shave (for the gents) every so often to maintain your facial hair too, and even dust off seats before you sit down. Do not wait for someone else to take responsibility for your cleanliness. It is a sign of irresponsibility on your part.

Cleanliness has immense benefits. Do you remember how you felt after taking that warm bath at the end of your busy day? How well were you received at your workstation when you showed up clean-shaven and well-groomed? Embracing cleanliness will open doors that character alone cannot.

4. Being Kind

A person's character is known from how they treat strangers, hotel attendants, public service vehicle operators, the needy in the streets, and those who have no means to repay them. Kindness is a habit, not an occasional act.

Make a point of being kind to those you meet every day. Do to others what you would like to be done to you. Karma is there to equalize the math. Kindness has no affiliation with being religious (although it is a doctrine in religion), but it is about being a better person. If you can donate to that charity event, do it generously. If you can clear the hospital bill of the sick, do it willingly. If you can pay fees for the needy students, kindly step in.

Make kindness your habit and generosity a part of you. It is not to mean that you become irrationally kind. Use rational judgment to distinguish between genuine and fake needy people. A simple act of kindness will change someone's life.

5. <u>Planning</u>

If you fail to plan, you are planning to fail. Planning arises from simple ignorable things. The not-so-petty matters that we overlook and comfort ourselves by saying it will not happen again. How often have we done impulse buying when shopping? It may look trivial but its impact on our finances cannot be overlooked.

Get your acts together and prioritize planning. Earn before you spend and save after you earn. Failure to plan will drive you to bankruptcy and depression. A good plan is a job half done. When you anticipate what will come next, you will be prepared to handle it effectively. That is what planning does to a man. It makes you a semi-god with the ability to come up with solutions to problems that are yet to come but are around the corner.

Isn't it adorable how powerful planning is? It is neither tedious as many see it nor reserved for the elite. A plan is essential for personal success.

6. <u>Learn Something New</u>

Knowledge is power. The best gift you can give yourself is to widen your knowledge base. Learn life hacks, human psychology and socializing. There are those lessons which cannot be taken in a classroom but out there in the real world. Take it upon yourself to learn something new daily.

Nothing is stagnant in the current world. Walk with the changes lest you be left behind. Adapt to new practices in your industry fast enough before most people do. Your flexibility will bring something to the table and you will attract greatness.

Learning something new daily is not solely academic. Regardless of your level of education, there is always something to learn. Do not despise those below you in the social ladder, you can always learn a thing or two.

7. Talk To At Least One Stranger

We all are reluctant to talk to strangers for one reason or another. We are worried about how they will respond to our greetings or maybe our proposals. One thing however is clear – strangers could be the potential turning point of our businesses and jobs. They could be the breakthrough we have been waiting for.

Pick up the courage to greet a stranger today and further a conversation. Be warned that some could be opportunists and exploit your goodwill. Nevertheless, talk to a stranger. Greet the people you find at the bus stage and the security guard at your place.

These 7 habits to do everyday are essential for personal growth.

Chapter 8:

The Downside of Work-Life Balance

One way to think about work-life balance is with a concept known as The Four Burners Theory. Here's how it was first explained to me:

Imagine that a stove represents your life with four burners on it. Each burner symbolizes one major quadrant of your life.

1. The first burner represents your family.

2. The second burner is your friends.

3. The third burner is your health.

4. The fourth burner is your work.

The Four Burners Theory says that "to be successful, you have to cut off one of your burners. And to be successful, you have to cut off two."

The View of the Four Burners

My initial reaction to The Four Burners Theory was to search for a way to bypass it. "Can I succeed and keep all four burners running?" I wondered.

Perhaps I could combine two burners. "What if I lumped family and friends into one category?"

Maybe I could combine health and work. "I hear sitting all day is unhealthy. What if I got a standing desk?" Now, I know what you are thinking. Believing that you will be healthy because you bought a standing desk is like believing you are a rebel because you ignored the fasten seatbelt sign on an airplane, but whatever.

Soon I realized I was inventing these workarounds because I didn't want to face the real issue: life is filled with tradeoffs. If you want to excel in your work and your marriage, then your friends and your health may have to suffer. If you want to be healthy and succeed as a parent, then you might be forced to dial back your career ambitions. Of course, you are free to divide your time equally among all four burners, but you have to accept that you will never reach your full potential in any given area.

Essentially, we are forced to choose. Would you rather live a life that is unbalanced but high-performing in a certain area? Or would you rather live a life that is balanced but never maximizes your potential in a given quadrant?

Option 1: Outsource Burners

We outsource small aspects of our lives all the time. We buy fast food, so we don't have to cook. We go to the dry cleaners to save time on laundry. We visit the car repair shop, so we don't have to fix our automobile.

Outsourcing small portions of your life allow you to save time and spend it elsewhere. Can you apply the same idea to one quadrant of your life and free up time to focus on the other three burners?

Work is the best example. For many people, work is the hottest burner on the stove. It is where they spend the most time, and it is the last burner to get turned off. In theory, entrepreneurs and business owners can outsource the work burner. They do it by hiring employees.

The Four Burners Theory reveals a truth everyone must deal with: nobody likes being told they can't have it all, but everyone has constraints on their time and energy. Every choice has a cost.

Which burners have you cut off?

Chapter 9:

7 Ways To Cultivate Emotions That Will Lead You To Greatness

Billions of men and women have walked the earth but only a handful have made their names engraved in history forever. These handful of people have achieved 'greatness' owing to their outstanding work, their passion and their character.

Now, greatness doesn't come overnight—greatness is not something you can just reach out and grab. Greatness is the result of how you have lived your entire life and what you have achieved in your lifetime. Against all your given circumstances, how impactful your life has been in this world, how much value you have given to the people around you, how much difference your presence has made in history counts towards how great you are. However, even though human greatness is subjective, people who are different and who have stood out from everyone else in a particular matter are perceived as great.

However, cultivating greatness in life asks for a 'great' deal of effort and all kinds of human effort are influenced by human emotions. So it's safe to say that greatness is, in fact, controlled by our emotions. Having said that, let's see what emotions are associated with greatness and how to cultivate them in real life:

1. Foster Gratitude

You cannot commence your journey towards greatness without being grateful first. That's right, being satisfied with what you already have in life and expressing due gratitude towards it will be your first step towards greatness. Being in a gratified emotional state at most times (if not all) will enhance your mental stability which will consequently help you perceive life in a different—or better point of view. This enhanced perception of life will remove your stresses and allow you to develop beyond the mediocrity of life and towards greatness.

2. Be As Curious As Child

Childhood is the time when a person starts to learn whatever that is around them. A child never stops questioning, a child never runs away from what they have to face. They just deal with things head on. Such kind of eagerness for life is something that most of us lose at the expense of time. As we grow up—as we know more, our interest keeps diminishing. We stop questioning anymore and accept what is. Eventually, we become entrapped into the ordinary. On the contrary, if we greet everything in life with bold eagerness, we expose ourselves to opportunities. And opportunities lead to greatness.

3. Ignite Your Passion

Passion has become a cliché term in any discussion related to achievements and life. Nevertheless, there is no way of denying the role of passion in driving your life force. Your ultimate zeal and fervor towards what you want in life is what distinguishes you to be great. Because admittedly, many people may want the same thing in life but how bad they want it—the intensity of wanting something is what drives people to stand out from the rest and win it over.

4. Become As Persistent As A Mountain

There are two types of great people on earth—1) Those who are born great and 2) Those who persistently work hard to become great. If you're reading this article, you probably belong to the later criteria. Being such, your determination is a key factor towards becoming great. Let nothing obstruct you—remain as firm as a mountain through all thick and thin. That kind of determination is what makes extraordinary out of the ordinary.

5. Develop Adaptability

As I have mentioned earlier, unless you are born great, your journey towards greatness will be an extremely demanding one. You will have to embrace great lengths beyond your comfort. In order to come out successful in such a journey, make sure that you become flexible to unexpected changes in your surroundings. Again, making yourself adaptable first in another journey in itself. You can't make yourself fit in adverse situations immediately. Adaptability or flexibility is cultivated prudently, with time, exposing yourself to adversities, little by little.

6.   Confidence Is Key

Road to greatness often means that you have to tread a path that is discouraged by most. It's obvious—by definition, everybody cannot be great. People will most likely advise against you when you aspire something out of the ordinary. Some will even present logical explanations against you;especially your close ones. But nothing should waver your faith. You must remain boldly confident towards what you're pursuing. Only you can bring your greatness. Believe that.

7.   Sense of Fulfilment Through Contributions

Honestly, there can be no greater feeling than what you'd feel after your presence has made a real impact on this world. If not, what else do we live for? Having contributed to the world and the people around you; this is the purpose of life. All the big and small contributions you make give meaning to your existence. It connects you to others, man and animal alike. It fulfills your purpose as a human being. We live for this sense of fulfillment and so, become a serial contributor. Create in yourself a greed for this feeling. At the end of the day, those who benefit from your contributions will revere you as great. No amount of success can be compared with this kind of greatness. So, never miss the opportunity of doing a good deed, no matter how minuscule or enormous.

In conclusion, these emotions don't come spontaneously. You have to create these emotions, cultivate them. And to cultivate these emotions, you must first understand yourself and your goals. With your eye on the prize, you have to create these emotions in you which will pave the path to your greatness. Gratitude, curiosity, passion, persistence, adaptability and fulfillment—each has its own weight and with all the emotions at play, nothing can stop you from becoming great in the truest form.

Chapter 10:

9 Habits of Highly Successful People

Success comes to people who deserve it. I bet you have heard this statement quite a few times, right? So, what does it mean exactly? Does it mean that you are either born worthy or unworthy of success? Absolutely not. Everyone is born worthy, but the one thing that makes some people successful is their winning habits and their commitment to these habits.

Today, we will learn how to master ten simple habits and behaviors that will help you become successful.

1. Be an Avid Learner

If you didn't know, almost all of the most successful people in the world are avid learners. So, do not shy away from opportunities when it comes to learning. Wake up each day and look forward to learning new things, and in no time, I bet you will experience how enriching it really is. Also, learning new things has the effect of revitalizing a person. So, if you want to have more knowledge to kickstart your journey in the right direction, here are some things that you can do - make sure to read, even if it is just a page or two, daily. It could be anything that interests you. I personally love reading self-help books. If you are not that much of a reader, you can even listen to a podcast, watch an informative video, or sign up for a course. Choose what piques your interest, and just dive into it!

2. Failure is the Pillar of Success

Most people are afraid to delve into something new, start a new chapter of their lives, and chase after their dreams – all because they are scared to fail. If you are one of those people who are scared to fail, well, don't be! Because what failure actually does is prepares you to achieve your dream. It just makes sure that you are able to handle the success when you finally have it. So when you accept that failure is an inevitable part of your journey, you will be able to plan the right course of action to tackle it instead of just being too scared to move forward. Successful people are never scared of failure; They just turn it around by seeing it as an opportunity to learn.

3. Get Up Early

I bet you have heard this a couple of thousand times already! But whoever told you so was not lying. Almost all successful individuals are early risers! They say that starting the morning right ensures a fruitful day ahead. It is true! Think about it, on the day you get up early, you feel a boost of productivity as compared to when you wake up late and have to struggle against the clock. You will have plenty of time and a good mood to go through the rest of the day which will give you better outcomes. All you have to do is set up a bedtime reminder. This is going to make sure that you enough rest to get up in the morning instead of snoozing your alarm on repeat! Not a morning person? Don't worry. I have got you covered! Start slow and set the alarm 15 minutes before when you usually wake up. It doesn't sound like much, eh? But trust me, you will be motivated to wake up earlier when you see how much difference 15 minutes can make to your day.

4. Have Your Own Morning Ritual

Morning rituals are the most common habit among achievers. It will pump you up to go through the day with a bang! You just have to make a routine for yourself and make sure to follow it every day. You can take inspiration from the morning routines of people you look up to but remember it has to benefit you. So you might be wondering, *What do I include in the ritual?* I would suggest you make your bed first thing in the morning. This might not sound as great a deal, but hey, it is a tested and approved method to boost your productivity. It is even implemented in the military. Doing this will motivate you as you get a sense of achievement as you have completed a task as soon as you woke up. After that, it could be anything that will encourage you, such as a walk, a workout session, reading, journaling, or meditating.

5. Stop Procrastinating

From delaying one task to not keeping up with your deadlines, procrastination becomes a deadly habit. It becomes almost unstoppable! Did you know, most people fail to achieve their dreams even if they have the potential just because of procrastination? Well, they do. And you might not want to become one of them. They say, "Old habits die hard," true, but they do die if you want them to. Procrastination has to be the hardest thing we have to deal with, even though we hey created it in the first place. Trust me, I speak from experience!

So what do you do to stop this? Break your task into small bite-sized pieces. Sometimes, it is just the heaviness of the task that keeps us from doing it. Take breaks in between to keep yourself motivated.

Another thing that you can do is the "minute rule." Divide your tasks by how much time they take. The tasks that take less than 5 minutes, you do it right then. Then you can bigger tasks into small time frames and complete them. Make sure you do not get too lost in the breaks, though!

6. Set Goals

I cannot even begin to tell you how effective goal setting is. A goal gives you the right direction and motivation. It also gives you a sense of urgency to do a task that is going to just take your productivity level from 0 to 10 in no time!

So how do you set goals? Simple. Think about the goals you want to achieve and write them down. But make sure that you set realistic goals. If you find it difficult, don't worry. Start small and slow. Start by making a to-do list for the day. You will find out soo that the satisfaction in ticking those off your list is unbelievable. It will also drive you to tick more of them off!

7. Make Your Health a Priority

Health is Wealth. Yes, it is a fact! When you give your body the right things and make it a priority, it gives you back by keeping you and your mind healthy. I bet you've heard the saying "You are what you eat," and by "eat," it does not simply mean to chew and swallow! It also means that you need to feed your body, soul, and mind with things you want them to be like. Read, listen, learn, and eat healthy. You could set a goal to eat clean for the week. Or workout at least for 10 minutes. And see for yourself how it gives you the energy to smash those goals you've been holding off! Also, great news – you can have cheat days once a week!

8. Plan Your Day the Night Before

"When you fail to plan, you plan to fail." People who succeed in life are not by mere coincidence or luck. It is the result of detailed, focused planning. So, you need to start planning your way to success too. Before you sleep tonight, ask yourself, *What is the most important thing that I have to do tomorrow?* Plan what assignments, meetings, or classes you have to complete. Planning ahead will not only make you organized and ready, it also highly increases your chances to succeed. So, don't forget to plan your day tonight!

9. Master the Habit Loop

Behavioral expert, BJ Fogg, explains that habits are formed around three elements: Cue, Routine, and Reward. Cue is the initial desire that motivates your behavior. Routine is the action you take. And the reward is the pleasure you gain after completion. So why am I telling you all of this? Because this habit loop is how we are wired. It is what motivates us. We seek pleasure and avoid pain. And you can use this loop to your advantage! Let's say you want to finish an assignment. Think of the reason why you want to. Maybe you don't want to fall behind someone or want to impress someone. It could be anything! Now time for you to set your rewards. It could be eating a slice of cheesecake or watching an episode of your favorite series after you've finished. Rewards motivate you when you slack off. Play around until you find a combination that works best for you. You will also need a cue; it could be anything like a notification on your phone, an email, or simply your desire. You can set a cue yourself by creating a reminder.

Habits are what make a man. I hope you follow these habits and start your journey the right way to becoming successful in life.

PART 2

Chapter 1:

How to Identify the Obstacles Holding You Back

Hi everyone! Have you ever wanted something in your life so badly but you failed to take any action to get it? Did you ever find out what was holding you back?

As humans, we have lots of aspirations and dreams. We strive to be rich and successful, pursuing our passions, having a big family, and living in a nice house with our dream car.
But how many of us were able to chase down that dream?

In today's video, we're going to talk about just that.

Let's find out how you can identify the obstacles holding us back from achieve your goals and how you can overcome them.

Before we begin, I would like you to first think about a goal you've been wanting to achieve but haven't started working on. If you're insightful, then ask yourself what are the possible reasons holding you back from working on it. Why are you procrastinating? Now that you've got something to latch on to, we can start to deconstruct the issues you might be facing.

1.   Fear of Failure

Most of the time, fear holds us back. Fear of failure is the most common fear that stops many people, including you and me, from working towards our intended goals. We are so afraid to fail after putting in an enormous amounts of time and effort, but we fail to realise that falling down is part of the process to victory. We do not see the struggles that many successful people have had to go through to get to where they are today – we only see the dollar signs that are tied to their name, their net-worth, their fancy houses and cars, things that are on face value. But in reality, they have had to fail their way to success. And we are oblivious to their trials and tribulations, their mindset, their incredible work ethic, and their ability to get themselves back up after falling flat on their faces and try again.

2.   Fear of Change

Another fear that could be holding you back from taking action is the fear of change. You may find it challenging to go out of your comfort zones to explore the big world of possibilities waiting for you. You may find your current position very safe, warm, and cosy. No stress, no pressure, just simply fine. But there's no growth in your comfort zone.

I am here to tell you that going out there to try new things isn't going to be easy. There may be a steep learning curve and a huge mountain waiting for you to climb. Are you willing to step out of that perfectly warmed home into a blizzard outside?

Putting yourself in uncomfortable situations is the only way that you will face challenges that might prove to be rewarding in the long run. Changes that will give you new perspectives and teach you new lessons that you wouldn't have learnt otherwise if you merely stay in your safe zone. So don't be afraid to go out in the world and try new things. No matter what the outcome is, the experiences you'll gain along the way will always be priceless.

3.   Fear of Judgement

Fear of being judged for doing things that are out of the norm is something that many of us are afraid of. In today's world, society has created a frame and a timeline of what seems to be pleasing and acceptable. Without realising it, we have been gradually moulded by society to try our best to blend into the crowd, not stand out. You may also inevitably feel that same pressure to simply just fit in. This irrational fear of being judged by others, whether it be our friends, family members, or even complete strangers, stops us in doing what we really want to do.

Now try to imagine yourself in a situation where other people won't judge you no matter what your dreams are. Instead, they will celebrate you for taking action and chasing your passions in life. If that were the reality, what will you do?

By reframing our thoughts, instead of succumbing to our desires of trying please everyone around us, we are thinking for ourselves first for once. There is no fear of judgement of pursuing what really matters to us. Don't be afraid to go out of that frame and restart. Listen to your own intuition and don't let the world put your hands on you and crush your dreams.

4. Fear of Making Mistakes

Are you the kind that always aces your test at school when you were young without studying? Or did you do well in school because you practiced a thousand times over before finally getting it right when it comes exam time?

You might think that having the perfect plan or having the perfect strategy is essential before you can begin executing your dreams, but in reality, a lot of the success only comes over time after many trials and errors. We have to keep the mindset that we will figure things out along the way as we travel down that new path. The journey will not be smooth sailing no matter how perfect we can try to make our plans to be. As with failures, making mistakes is part of the game. It is how you react to and manage the problems that come up that will be the true test of your capabilities.

Perfectionism is a trap that stops us from doing what we want. Doing something imperfectly is so much better than not doing anything at all because of the fear of imperfection.

5. Having a Weak Mindset

Another factor that holds people back is their own mindset. Have you ever wanted to try something out but you instantly think that you can't do it? The thought that you are incapable of something is all in your mind. You must tell yourself that you are flexible and fluid. That you are able to achieve anything you set your mind to.

That you have what it takes to go after the life that you want. The truth is, you have everything within you to be successful if you'll just believe that you can. Every time you catch yourself thinking that you can't be who you want to be, the reality is not that you can't do it, but rather that you just simply don't want to do it – either out of laziness or out of the fears that we have described so far.

To change your life you first have to change your mindset and be open to all possibilities.

6. Blaming Others Your Shortcomings

It is human nature to blame others for things that we lack or fail to do. We may direct our failure to take action to our circumstances, our environment, our lack of resources, or even our parents.

Blaming everything and everyone around you for your circumstances will hinder you from moving forward. Instead, be accountable for your own progress. We all have a choice to look at ourselves first and find the shortcomings that we may have. It could be a lack of motivation, lack of perseverance, , lack of patience, lack of consistency, and lack of discipline that is holding you back.

It is time to stop looking at external factors as reasons for our inability to take action. We all need to start working on ourselves first before we can see real change and progress happen to our lives. If you don't want where you are right now, do something about it. Move heaven and earth if you must. Don't stop until you reach where you want to be.

Closing.

Knowing what's holding you back is the first step you need to take to overcome them. Acknowledge these blockers and work on them. If you are afraid to fail, remember that failure is just part of the whole journey. If you are afraid of the uncertainties, remember that all our choices are half chances. And if we are afraid that we might just be wasting time, remember that whatever the outcome that your learning and experiences will make all your effort worth it in the end. You are not defined by the amount of effort you put in, not your failures.

I hope this video inspires you to always choose to look at things positively and outgrow whatever hinders you. No matter what your circumstances are, you have the power to turn things around and succeed. Many people have done it and trust that you can also do it. If you like this video, please give it a thumbs up and subscribe for more.

Chapter 2:

10 Habits of Jack Ma

It takes a special person to amass a total net worth of more than $20 billion through hard work and keeping a sense of perspective. Alibaba, one of world's largest e-commerce online platforms, Ceo and founder, Jack Ma is one of the world's wealthiest people, but his success hasn't clouded his strategic direction. Jack Ma's success habits will truly inspire you whether you are an aspiring billionaire or you're a small-business entrepreneur.

To grow his e-commerce business, Jack overcame all difficulties. He had a rough upbringing in communist China. He also failed the college admissions exams twice and was turned down by more than a dozen businesses. He had previously created two failed Internet businesses. However, the third time, Alibaba took off swiftly.

Here are 10 things you can grasps from Jack Ma success journey:

1. Giving Up is Failing

Jack Ma is one person who understands the meaning of failure, as it started in his early days. He founded two companies which terribly failed before the success of Alibaba. For Ma, giving up is failure.

Give your grind your best shot even when the struggle is real. Failing shouldn't make you give up, instead make sure you see the goal through to the end. Hardship is your learning lesson, and understanding its lessons is the key to fortune.

2. Let Your Initiative Impact on Society Positively

Ma created his vision focusing on its impactful influence on consumers. He also notes that consumer's happiness should be the end goal rather than the profits.

Let your entrepreneurial path be the reason why people's lives are improving. This results will be in long-term-positive business relationships.

3. What's Matters Is Where You Finish

Your humble beginnings shouldn't prevent you from taking chances. Your spirit, toughness, grit, and fortitude will tell whether or not you'll succeed.

What matters is whether you are putting much effort as needed and this will tell how determined you are to succeed. Dig in your heels, like Jack Ma, and give every opportunity your all.

4. Act Swiftly

According to Jack Ma, you must be extremely quick in seizing opportunities. To win in the end, you must first be off the starting line. You must also be quick to recover from and learn from mistakes. Grab an opportunity that is in your line of sight as soon as you see it and work with it before anyone else does. This will elevate you above your competitors, who are merely competent.

5. Persistence

Ma believes that leaders must be tenacious and with a clear vision. Understanding what you want and having the drive to pursue it will not only put you on the path to success, but will also inspire those around you to work hard to achieve their goals. Ma's business concept is around taking pleasure in one's job and refusing to accept no for an answer.

6. Foresightedness

A good leader, according to Jack Ma, should have foresight. As a leader, it's good that you're always one step ahead of the competition by anticipating how decisions will be implemented before others. Invest your time in developing creative strategies while intensifying a trait where you always follow a knowledge-based intuition.

7. Take a risk

Ma founded Alibaba Group, a very successful conglomerate of internet enterprises, in the face of skepticism from potential investors. The perfect time to take risks, is when you are pursuing your chosen goal path-when criticism is at its core.

8. Be Prepared to Fail

Jack Ma is no stranger to failure. He applied to college three times before being accepted. He created two unsuccessful companies before success of Alibaba. Even KFC didn't think he was a good fit.

When you give up on your first try, you are turning your life around. As probably you'll move on to something else while ending your dreams.

9. Take Chances When You're Still Young

Ma believes that if you are not wealthy by the age of 35, you have squandered your youth. Take use of your youth's vitality and imagination by succumbing to your goal and pursuing it.

Accept and learn from every opportunity that comes your way while you're still young. Grab every opportunity and make best of it by giving it your all. Your ability to pick up any job will help you develop tenancy.

10. Live life

Ma has a reputation for not taking things too seriously. Despite his hectic schedule, he always finds time to relax and enjoy life. If you work your whole life, you will undoubtedly come to regret it.

Conclusion

Jack Ma is one of most inspiring person in the world. His struggle way up and desire for wealth continues to inspire. Through his experience, Jack Ma demonstrates how as an entrepreneur, you can bring ambition to life.

Chapter 3:
7 Ways To Remove Excess Noise In Your Life

Ever felt lost in a world that is so fast-paced, where no two moments are the same? Do you ever have a hard time achieving your goals, just because you have more distractions than a purpose to jump to success?

We live in a time, where technology is the biggest ease as well as the biggest difficulty while achieving our goals.

When you need something to be fixed, the internet can save us a lot of time, but the same internet can prove to be the biggest cause to take away the focus of the most determined too.

Although there are many important things on the internet too, that are essential to our daily lives, we don't need them at all times. Especially the realm of social media platforms.

Youtube, Facebook even Instagram can prove to be a beneficial tool for learning and teaching. But it can also make you spend more and more time on things that won't give you much except a good laugh here and there.

So what habits or activities can you adapt to distill these distractions. Reduce noise in life helping you focus better on the things that matter the most.

1. Divide your Tasks Into Smaller Ones

When you already have many distractions in life, including the household tasks and other daily life chores that you must attend to, then you must not avoid those.

But your dreams and goals must not be put aside at all, instead one must learn to complete them by dividing them into smaller, more manageable tasks.

Those who depend on you must have you when they need you, but that shouldn't stop you from doing what you require from yourself.

That can be done by keeping your head in the work whenever you get the chance to get maximum results from those short intervals.

2. Manage Your Time Smartly

Life is too short to be indulging in every whim and activity that you crave. Not everything or thought requires you to act upon.

A human being is the smartest being on this planet but also the stupidest. When a man or a woman wants to achieve something with all their heart, they do get it eventually. But when they have a thousand silly desires to go for, they slide off the set path as if there were none.

"You only Live Once".

Logically, this is a valid quote to get anyone off their path to success. But, realistically this is also the most common reason for the failure of a majority of our youngsters.

You only get this life once, So you must go for the acts that bring you a better future with a surety of freedom without having to rely on anyone. Life doesn't need to be a continuous struggle once you use your energies at the right time for the right time.

3. Get Your Head Out of Social Media

I know this may sound a little Grownup and cliched, but we spend more time on our mobiles and laptops than going out and doing something physically in all our senses with our actual hands.

We can believe and act on anything that pops up on this screen but rarely do we get anything worthwhile that we can adapt to change our lives once and for all.

Social media might be the new medium and source of knowledge and business for many, but for a layman, this is also the biggest waste of creative energy.

There is a lot out there to do in real life, a lot that we can realistically achieve. But, these days, we tend to hide behind a simple tweet and believe that we have done enough when the reality could have been much different.

4. Avoid Unhealthy Relationships

You might have always heard that a friend can be an emotional escape when you need one, but the excess of friends can prove to be the opposite of that. People seem to think, the more friends you have, the better you have a chance to stay engaged and have a happy social life. But this isn't always the case.

The more you have friends, your devotion gets scattered and you find solace in everyone's company. This makes you more exposed, and people might take advantage of that. The fewer friends you have, the better loyalty you can expect and better returns of a favor.

When you have fewer friends, even if you lose one someday or get deceived, you would require less time to bounce back from the incident and you won't have to worry for long.

5. Get Out of Home Environment

Productivity required a productive environment. People tend to look for ease, but it doesn't always help us with finding our true potential.

You sometimes need a strict office environment or a more organized station or workplace. A place where there is no distraction or source of wandering thoughts to get your attention.

People need to understand how our brains work. If you cannot focus sitting in your bed, get a chair and a table. If that doesn't work for you, take a stool without a backrest. If you still feel at ease, just pick a standing table and start working while standing on your feet.

This makes your mind stay more focused on the task at hand to be done quickly.

6. Make A Schedule For These Distractions

If you feel like you can't give up the urge to pick your phone and check your feed. Or if you need to watch the last quarter of the league, Or if you need to have a smoke.

Don't start fighting these urges. It won't help you, rather make things worse.

If you cannot let go off of these things, it's fine. Make a deal with your brain, that you need this last page done within the next 10 minutes, and then I can go do what I needed direly.

You have to come at peace with your mind and work as a single unit. So make time for these distractions and gradually you might be able to drop them once and for all.

7. You Don't Have to Compare With Anyone

Why do we humans need to compare and compete? Because we think it keeps our drive and our struggle alive. We think it gives us a reason and a purpose to go on and makes us see our goals more clearly.

Comparing to others won't make you see 'Your Goals', rather you would start creating goals that were never meant to be for you. You have these priorities just because you saw someone with something that appealed to you.

This is the noise and distraction that deviates you from the path that was meant to be for you all along.

If you want a clear vision of what you want, start removing cluttered thoughts, acts, and people from your life. It might seem hard at the start, but you won't have any regrets once everything comes in place.

Chapter 4:

10 Habits of Rafael Nadal

Rafael Nadal is a Spanish professional tennis player famously known as "The King of Clay" because of his dominance and success on the tennis court. He is currently ranked No. 4 in the world by the ATP, with previous records as No. 1 in the ATP rankings for 209 weeks, and has closed the year as No. 1 five times.

Great champions are born with the ability to persevere in the face of adversity, including fear, suffering, self-doubt, and helplessness. Rafael Nadal proved this yet again by fighting like a gladiator to win his 13th French Open title and 20th Major overall at the just-concluded Roland Garros event. You don't achieve that kind of reputation unless you're continuously humble, hardworking, and producing exceptional outcomes.

Here are ten habits of Rafael Nadal.

1. Neurotic on-Court Habits

Before every match, Nadal has made it a habit of taking cold showers, towels down after even aces, and double points. He points the labels of his drinking bottles at the end of the court he's about to play from and never stands up from his chair before his opponent. If you're not this neurotic, you'll never made it to the Wimbledon Final.

2. Trophies Are a Product of Well-Earned Practice

Despite your incredible athlete talents and abilities, as Rafael notes, is not enough to secure a win over 13 French Opens. But careful and intensive practice does. His workout routine is based on Anders Ericsson's "10,000-hour rule" for court success.

3. Focus

Alongside hard work, you need focus. Rafa plays every point as if his life depends on it. Extraordinary outcomes depend on your concentration on winning points.

4. Every Strike Counts

Rafael is constantly putting himself in the best winning position for each point, game, and set. Rafael on his serve says: "It's not just about your serving ideas but also your positioning, speed variation, and spin." It definitely gets better!

5. Be Self-Assured

Nadal is not of those athletes who focus on self-doubt thoughts even while going against a competitive rival on the court. Self-confidence is the most crucial variable in sports and performance psychology.

6. Excellence Is a Habit

Work hard every day; as Rafa puts it, when you wake up motivated to intense workout and practice, you'll always excel in your performance tactics. Rafa understands that the most challenging work begins right before his next match, and he has one goal, "enjoy your game while playing, and always strive on improving."

7. You Can't Succeed on Your Own

No matter your dedicated you are, you never win anything on your own. For the same reason, Nadal always has his Uncle Toni, his family, and friends by his side. Uncle Toni has taught him how to be mentally tough to succeed. To become an elite athlete, you'll have to learn and practice patience, put up with whatever comes your way, overcome weakness and agony, and push yourself to the limit.

8. Serve Others

In 2008 he launched the Rafa Nadal Foundation, known for its social and personal aid for less in Spain and India. He believes sport opens the doors to a better future. Becoming a star is one thing, but portraying your humanity trait makes it better.

9. Grit

Angela Lee defines grit as "passion and tenacity for very long-term goals." Grit is endurance and commitment to your future. As a tennis player, you can win and lose, and you must be prepared for both. However, as you get older, both winning and losing become easier. That is what characterizes Nadal's tennis. In every match, whether he wins or loses, his will and determination to battle till the end distinguish him.

10. Tournaments End. Dedication, Does Not

When you're down two sets, remember to keep calm, even when people cheering you up are freaking out and worried about you. According to Rafa, "the only way to achieve this is to fight back, move, run, and control that pressure." Every time Rafa enters the court, he leaves with a new found hunger and gives his all in every point, regardless of whether he is playing against a qualifier or the greatest of all.

Conclusion

Rafa plays hard wherever and whenever he plays. He is adamant. He is tenacious and plays for the love of the game. You may argue that all records are supposed to be broken, and all athletic events are just games. Still, they're also about leaving a legacy, accepting and expressing pride in one's abilities.

Chapter 5:

8 Ways to Discover What's holding You Back From Achieving Your Visions

We all have dreams, and I have no questions; you have made attempts at seeking after your goals. Oh, as a general rule, life's battles get the better of you and keep you down. The pressure of everyday life, again and again, puts you down. Regardless of your determination, devotion, and want, alone, they are not enough.

Being here exhibits you are not able to settle for a mediocre life and hidden desires. To help you in your goal of seeking after your objectives, you must become acquainted with those things keeping you down. When you do, you will want to eliminate every single reason keeping you down.

1. Fear

The deep-rooted foe is very likely a critical factor in keeping many of you from seeking after your objectives. It prevents you from acting, making you scared of venturing out. Dread is the thing that keeps you down. Dread is one reason why we don't follow what we truly need throughout everyday life.

• Fear of disappointment
• Fear of dismissal

• Fear of mocking

• Fear of disappointment

Quit allowing your feelings of fear to keep you down!

2. Procrastination

Putting things off till the following week, one month from now, one year from now, and regularly forever. You're not exactly sure the thing you're hanging tight for, but rather when whatever it happens, you'll be prepared to start seeking after your objectives. Be that as it may, this day never comes. Your fantasy stays as just a fantasy. Putting things off can just keep you down.

Quit allowing your Procrastination to keep you down!

3. Justifications

Do you find yourself procrastinating and making excuses for why you can't start working toward your goals? Those that succeed in accomplishing their objectives can overcome obstacles. So many individuals make excuses for themselves, believing they can't achieve a better career, start their own business, or find their ideal lifemate.

• It isn't the correct time

• I am insufficient

 • I am too old/young

Don't allow your excuses to hold you back any longer!

4. Lack of Confidence

Lack of confidence in yourself or your ability to achieve your goals will inevitably hold you back. Our actions, or lack thereof, are influenced by what goes on in our subconscious mind. We have self-limiting and negative beliefs that may be preventing us from enjoying an extraordinary life.

Nothing will be able to stop you if you believe in yourself. Bringing your limiting beliefs into focus will help you achieve your objectives.

Don't let your lack of confidence keep you back!

5. There Isn't A Big Picture

Others refer to what I call a breakthrough goal as a BHAG - Big Hairy Audacious Goal. A goal is what you need to keep you motivated and drive you to achieve it every day. Start small and dream big. You'll need a strong enough passion to propel you forward. Your ambitions will not motivate you until you first dream big.

For your objectives to be beneficial to you, they must assist you in realizing your ambitions. Those lofty ambitions. Goals can only motivate you, help you stay focused, and help you make the adjustments you need to make, as well as provide you the fortitude to overcome difficulties as you chase your big-picture dreams if they matter to you.

Stop allowing your big picture to stifle your progress!

6. Inability To Concentrate

Your chances of success are slashed every moment you lose focus. When we spread our focus too thin, we dilute our effort and lose the ability to focus on the most significant tasks. When you're pulled in a lot of different directions and have a lot of conflicting priorities fighting for your attention, it's easy to lose track of what's important. Any attempts to achieve vital goals will be harmed as a result of this.

Stop allowing your lack of concentration to keep you back!

7. Failure to Make a Plan

Finally, if you don't have a strategy, it's easy to become lost along the route. Consider driving across the country without a map, say from London to Glasgow. While you have a rough route in mind, there are many lands to cover and a lot of false turns and dead ends to be avoided. You can get there with the help of a GPS. It plots your path and creates a plan for you. A plan provides you with the road map you need to reach your objectives. This is the process of determining what you need to accomplish to reach your objectives. This is where you put in the time and effort to write out a plan of the steps you need to follow, the resources you'll need, and the amount of time you'll need to invest.

Stop allowing the lack of a strategy holds you back!

8. Not Keeping Track of Your Progress and Making Necessary Modifications

Goals, by their very nature, take time to attain. Therefore it's critical to keep track of your progress. You won't know what's working and what's not if you don't get quick and actionable feedback. You won't be able to tell when to alter or when to keep doing what you're doing. Anyone who is continuously successful in accomplishing their goals also reviews their goals and progress regularly. Regularly reviewing your goals allows you to make early modifications to stay on track.

Stop allowing not reviewing and adjusting your progress to hold you back!

Chapter 6:

7 Habits To Change Your Life

Consistently, habit drives you to do what you do—regardless of whether it's a matter of considerations or conduct that happens naturally. Whatever that is, imagine a scenario where you could saddle the power of your habits to improve things. Envision a day to day existence where you have a habit for finishing projects, eating admirably, staying in contact with loved ones, and working to your fullest potential. At the point when you have an establishment of beneficial routines, you're setting yourself up for a full, sound, and effective life.

Here are 7 habits that Can change your entire life.

1. Pinpoint and Focus Entirely on Your Key stone Routine.

Charles Duhigg, in his power book stipulates the essence of recognizing your Keystone Habit—the habit you distinguish as the main thing you can change about your life. To discover what that is for you, ask yourself, what continually worries you? Is it something you would that you like to stop, or something you would do and prefer not to begin? The cornerstone habit is distinctive for everybody, and it might take a couple of meetings of profound thought to pinpoint precisely what that habit is.

Whichever propensity you're chipping away at, pick each in turn. More than each in turn will be overpowering and will improve your probability of neglecting to improve any habits. Be that as it may, don't really accept that you can just change one thing about yourself; it's really the inverse. Dealing with this one Keystone Habit can have a positive gradually expanding influence into the remainder of your life also.

2. Recognize Your Present Daily Practice and the Reward You Get From It

Suppose you need to fabricate a habit for getting to the workplace a half hour early every day. You need to do this since you figured the extra peaceful time in the morning hours will assist you with being more gainful, and that profitability will be compensated by an expanded feeling of occupation fulfilment, and a generally speaking better workplace. As of now, you get to the workplace simply on schedule. Your present routine is to take off from your home in a hurry, at the specific time you've determined that (without traffic or episode) will get you to chip away at time. Your award is investing some additional energy at your home in the first part of the day, spending an additional half hour dozing or "charging your batteries" for the day ahead.

3. Take the Challenges Into Consideration.

Challenges are regularly prompts that push you to fall once more into old habits. In the case of having to get to work earlier, your challenges may lie in your rest designs the prior night, or in organizing plans with a partner. These difficulties won't mysteriously vanish so you need to consider them. In any case, don't let the presence of challenges, or stress that new difficulties will come up later on, discourage you from setting up your new propensities. In the event that your difficulties incorporate planning with others, make them a piece of your new daily practice, as I'll clarify later. At this moment, basically recognize what the difficulties or obstructions are.

4. Plan and Identifying Your New Routine.

Old habits never vanish; they are basically supplanted with new propensities. In the case of getting to the workplace earlier, the new standard includes going out a half hour sooner. On the off chance that the old habit was remunerated with the possibility that you'll have more energy for the day by remaining in your home longer, the new propensity needs to centre around the possibility that more rest doesn't really mean more energy. All in all, you'll need to address what you think you'll be surrendering by supplanting the old habit.

5. Reinforce a 30 Days Challenge.

By and large, your inability to minister beneficial routines basically comes from not adhering to them. A lot of studies show that habits, when performed day by day, can turn out to be important for your daily schedule in just 21 days. So set a beginning date and dispatch your game plan for a preliminary 30-day time span.

6. Empower Your Energy Through Setbacks

Here and there, it's not simply self-control that runs out. Now and then you are influenced from your ways by life "hindering" new objectives. In the event that something influences you from your test, the best game-plan is to assess the circumstance and perceive how you can get around, finished, or through that deterrent. Notwithstanding, when another propensity is set up, it really turns into our default setting. Assuming your standard habits are sound, unpleasant occasions are less inclined to lose you from your typical schedules. All in all, we're similarly prone to default to solid habits as we are to self-undermining habits, if those sound habits have become a piece of our ordinary daily practice.

7. Account Yourself and for Your Actions P ublicly (Hold Yourself Accountable).

Your encouraging people are the most significant asset you will have at any point. Regardless of whether it's your closest companion, your accomplice or your Facebook posts, being responsible to somebody other than yourself will help you adhere to your objective. Simply remember that "responsible" isn't equivalent to "declaration". Anybody can advise the world they will rise ahead of schedule from here on out. However, on the off chance that that individual has a group of allies behind them, whom they routinely update, they are bound to stay with their new propensity during times when they are building up their new habit and inspiration is coming up short.

Chapter 7:

The Power of Developing Eye Contact with Your Client

We've all heard the age-old saying the "eyes are the window to the soul," and in many ways, it holds. Everybody knows looking others in the eyes is beneficial in communication, but how important is eye contact, and how is it defined?

Eye contact can be subtle or even obvious. It can be a glaring scowl when a person is upset or a long glance when we see something off about someone else's appearance. It can even be a direct look when we are trying to express a crucial idea.

1) Respect

In Western countries like the United States, eye contact is critical to show and earn respect. From talking to your boss on the job or thanking your mom for dinner, eye contact shows the other person that you feel equal in importance.

There are other ways to show respect, but our eyes reflect our sincerity, warmth, and honesty.

This is why giving and receiving eye contact while talking is a surefire sign of a good conversation. Nowadays, it's common for people to glance at their phones no matter if they're in the middle of a conversation or not. That's why eye contact will set you apart and truly show that you give them your full and undivided attention.

2) Understanding

Sometimes locking glances is the only sign you need to show someone that you understand what they are talking about. More specifically, if you need to get a vital point across, eye contact is the best way to communicate that importance. Eye contact is also a form of background acknowledgment like saying "yeah" and "mhmm."

That means it shows the speaker that you are tuned in to and understand what they are saying.

3) Bonding

When someone is feeling an emotion or just performing a task, the same neurons that shine in their brain light up in someone else's brain who is watching them. This is because we have "mirror neurons" in our brains that are very sensitive to facial expressions and, most importantly, eye contact.

Direct eye contact is so powerful that it increases empathy and links together emotional states. Never underestimate the power of eye contact in creating long-lasting bonds.

4) Reveal Thoughts and Feelings

We have countless ways of describing eyes, including "shifty-eyed," "kind-eyed," "bright-eyed," "glazed over," and more. It's no wonder just about every classic love story starts with "two pairs of eyes meeting across the room." Eye contact is also a powerful form of simultaneous communication, meaning you don't have to take turns doing the communicating.

Ever wonder why poker players often wear sunglasses inside? It's because "the eyes don't lie." We instinctually look into people's eyes from birth to try and understand what they are thinking, and we continue to do it for life.

Chapter 8:

10 Habits to Start Right Now

Have you ever wondered why you are not able to achieve your goals and aspirations? You might get a little confused while searching for the stumbling block on the way to your success, but the answer is simple and right in front of you. It is procrastination and some other unhealthy habits.

Here are ten healthy habits that you need to start incorporating in your life immediately.

1. Maintaining a Routine

You can't expect that everything will be in order one fine morning and you will start achieving all your goals suddenly just like that. It doesn't work that way. Success comes when you start taking small steps every day and slowly work on your progress little by little. You need to start to maintain a routine regularly. Doing this will help you get rid of your procrastination. You can start with simple things like doing some household chores like cooking, cleaning, etc. Let's say you have decided to cook every day – whenever you think that you need to cook all three meals and for everyone, it might intimidate you. You can start with small tasks that are more manageable. So, start with cooking an item every day. That won't take much time and won't be that difficult either – once you start doing this, start increasing the amount and intensity of the work. After you understand how this routine thing works, you can slowly move towards the work related to your goals and aspirations and maintain a routine.

2. Embracing Immediacy

Most people like to put things aside for doing those later. It is a huge mistake that can have serious consequences. People procrastinate everything like problematic things, easy things, small things, big things, and fun things. When you put aside something for doing it later, it gets more challenging to do with time. So, you just keep pushing it further and further until there is no time left to do it. You can overcome this by immediacy. Whenever you are reminded or informed about some work, start doing it immediately and don't keep it pending for later. If it is a small thing that requires a little time to finish, then make sure to finish it in one go. If it is a long work, start working immediately and take breaks and work whenever possible.

3. React Thoughtfully

Most people allow their emotions to control their reactions. Try to avoid making decisions while your emotions are heightened. This is because the decisions that are taken while emotions are heightened are usually wrong decisions and can have detrimental consequences. Your heightened emotions make you blind, and you do things that you wouldn't have done otherwise. So, whenever something triggers you, don't let your gut reaction out. Wait for some time, probably 5-6 minutes, and then act. When you give yourself a little time, it allows you to see through the situation and think beyond those overwhelming emotions. It will make you see the bigger picture and react thoughtfully.

4. Quitting Clicks, Swipes, and Scrolls

Do you even realize how much time you spend aimlessly clicking, swiping, or scrolling? It wastes a lot of your time and is also responsible for draining your productivity, concentration, and motivation. A little bit of digital media does no harm. It is, in fact, helpful because you can get loads of information from the media. But if you keep scrolling for hours, that is where the problem begins. You need to cut down on your use of media to allow yourself to get benefitted from it. If you find difficulty reducing the use of media by yourself, you can try using a browser blocker. It will block all the media outlets after a specified amount of time, thereby limiting the time you spend over there.

5. Embracing the Old

It is usual for people to crave new things every time. But sometimes, people get so overwhelmed by the excitement of trying to gain something new that they forget to cherish the things they already have in their possession. Gaining something you wanted to can be a little exciting and fun for some time, but this will just feed your urge to gain more and more things. Most people already possess everything they require, but they don't seem to see it because of the urge to get something new. For example, a person having a closet full of clothes keeps on buying new clothes every time he has somewhere to go. If you find yourself in a similar situation, you can avoid this by looking at the closet carefully and observing everything you have in your possession. You can, maybe, rearrange the closet in a way where you will be able to see stuff the way you want to see. Once you start cherishing the things that you already have, you can go a long way.

6. Remember Your Achievements

Sometimes, you are too harsh on yourself, and you blame yourself way too much. You should always treat yourself with the same amount of kindness and positivity you possess while treating others. Everyone has their fair share of successes and failures in their lives. So, you should be grateful for everything you achieved and not take those for granted. Instead of regretting and blaming yourself for the things you couldn't achieve, try reminding yourself amount the things you actually did achieve. Appreciate yourself for every good thing that you have done in your life. It can be something like quitting certain habits, scoring certain marks in an exam, doing something good for others, etc. So, whenever you make some mistake, you need to remind yourself of all the small and big things you have achieved so that you don't get too disheartened to get up and move on. Embrace the good in you!

7. Declutter

Have you ever felt that whenever you change the orientation of the furniture in your room, you get excited and feel different? This is because even a tiny change is considered to be new, fun, and exciting. Your motivation and productivity get hugely affected by your workspace environment. If your workspace environment is messy, it is going to inspire your creativity subconsciously. In contrast, if you have a well-organized workspace, it will subconsciously boost your efficiency and help you remove any mental clutter. Keep changing your workspace from time to time. Keep it messy somedays, for increasing your creativity levels. When you need to do a lot of hard work that demands efficiency, arrange everything in order and make your workspace well-organized. You can add some photo frames to give it a different and exciting look.

8. Set Small Achievable Goals Everyday

People feel the most satisfied when they know that they have achieved a certain goal. You can use it to your advantage for brightening up your day. Set small achievable goals throughout your day so that you can easily achieve them. It can be as simple as making your bed after you get up, and so on. Make sure that you already have 2-3 achieved goals before you have your breakfast. These small benchmarks play a vital role in kick-starting your day on a good note. All these little benchmarks add up and give you a sense of pride and satisfaction after you achieve them, thereby brightening up your day.

9. Give Compliments

People love to receive compliments from others but get a little shaky while giving compliments to others. Have you ever wondered why? It is probably because you worry about how it would make you look like. You feel that complimenting others can make you look lighter and easy. That's absolutely not the case. Complimenting people can really help you start a conversation with different people and get friendly. It is a fantastic social skill that you need to learn because of the various benefits it offers. Don't fear what others will think, and don't sugarcoat your words either. Because when you give fake compliments, people can feel that it is not coming from your heart, leaving a very negative impression on them. Try to be as genuine as possible and speak your mind out.

10. Commit to Relaxation

A lot of people work continuously, and even when they are taking a break, all they think about is their work! It is not a healthy habit and needs to be changed immediately. When you work yourself too much and don't give yourself the amount of relaxation it deserves, work seems to be more complicated than it actually is, thereby reducing your productivity and concentration. When you feel like you can't work anymore and that you have reached your threshold cut yourself some slack! When you are taking a break, make sure not to think about work at all. Plan something relaxing, exciting, or fun, and enjoy yourself fully while taking some time off from your work. It will recharge your mind, and then you can return to your work, being energetic and positive.

I hope you follow these steps and develop them as habits in your daily life so that you can make the most out of your life and stay happy.

Chapter 9:

8 Steps To Develop Beliefs That Will Drive you To Success

'Success' is a broad term. There is no universal definition of success, it varies from person to person considering their overall circumstances. We can all more or less agree that confidence plays a key role in it, and confidence comes from belief.

Even our most minute decisions and choices in life are a result of believing in some specific outcome that we have not observed yet.

However, merely believing in an ultimate success will not bring fortune knocking at your door. But, it certainly can get you started—take tiny steps that might lead you towards your goal. Now, since we agree that having faith can move you towards success, let's look at some ways to rewire your brain into adopting productive beliefs.

Here are 8 Steps to Develop Beliefs That Will Drive You To Success:

1. Come Up With A Goal

Before you start, you need to decide what you want to achieve first. Keep in mind that you don't have to come up with something very specific right away because your expectations and decisions might change over time. Just outline a crude sense of what 'Achievement' and 'Success' mean to you in the present moment.

Begin here. Begin now. Work towards getting there.

2. Put Your Imagination Into Top Gear

"Logic will take you from A to B. Imagination will take you everywhere", said Albert Einstein.

Imagination is really important in any scenario whatsoever. It is what makes us humans different from animals. It is what gives us a reason to move forward—it gives us hope. And from that hope, we develop the will to do things we have never done before.

After going through the first step of determining your goal, you must now imagine yourself being successful in the near future. You have to literally picture yourself in the future, enjoying your essence of fulfilment as vividly as you can. This way, your ultimate success will appear a lot closer and realistic.

3. Write Notes To Yourself

Writing down your thoughts on paper is an effective way to get those thoughts stuck in your head for a long time. This is why children are encouraged to write down what is written in the books instead of memorizing them just by reading. You have to write short, simple, motivating notes to yourself that will encourage you to take actions towards your success. It doesn't matter whether you write in a notebook, or on your phone or wherever—just write it. On top of that, occasionally read what you've written and thus, you will remain charged with motivation at all times.

4. Make Reading A Habit

There are countless books written by successful people just so that they can share the struggle and experience behind their greatest achievements. In such an abundance of manuscripts, you may easily find books that portray narratives similar to your life and circumstances. Get reading and expand your knowledge. You'll get never-thought-before ideas that will guide you through your path to success. Reading such books will tremendously strengthen your faith in yourself, and in your success. Read what other successful people believed in—what drove them. You might even find newer beliefs to hold on to. No wonder why books are called 'Man's best friend'.

5. Talk To People Who Motivates You

Before taking this step, you have to be very careful about who you talk to. Basically, you have to speak out your goals and ambitions in life to someone who will be extremely supportive of you. Just talk to them about what you want, share your beliefs and they will motivate you from time to time towards success. They will act as powerful reminders.

Being social beings, no human can ever reject the gist of motivation coming from another human being—especially when that is someone whom you can rely on comfortably. Humans have been the sole supporter of each other since eternity.

6. Make A Mantra

Self-affirming one-liners like 'I can do it', 'Nothing can stop me', 'Success is mine' etc. will establish a sense of firm confidence in your subconscious mind. Experts have been speculative about the power of our subconscious mind for long. The extent of what it can do is still beyond our grasp. But nonetheless, reciting subtle mantras isn't a difficult task. Do it a couple of times every day and it will remain in your mind for ages, without you giving any conscious thought to it. Such subconscious affirmations may light you up in the right moment and show you the path to success when you least expect it.

7. Reward Yourself From Time To Time

Sometimes, your goals might be too far-fetched and as a result, you'll find it harder to believe in something so improbable right now. In a situation like this, what you can do is make short term objectives that ultimately lead to your main goal and for each of those objectives achieved, treat yourself with a reward of any sort—absolutely anything that pleases you. This way, your far cry success will become more apparent to you in the present time. Instant rewards like these will also keep you motivated and make you long for more. This will drive you to believe that you are getting there, you are getting closer and closer to success.

8. Having Faith In Yourself

Your faith is in your hands alone. How strongly you believe in what you deserve will motivate you. It will steer the way for self-confidence to fulfill your inner self. You may be extremely good at something but due to the lack of faith in your own capabilities, you never attempted it—how will you ever know that you were good at that? Your faith in yourself and your destined success will materialize before you through these rewards that you reserve for yourself. You absolutely deserve this!

Final Thoughts

That self-confidence and belief and yourself, in your capabilities and strengths will make you work towards your goal. Keep in mind that whatever you believe in is what you live for. At the end of the day, each of us believed in something that made us thrive, made us work and move forward. Some believed in the military, some believed in maths, some believed in thievery—everyone had a belief which gave them a purpose—the purpose of materializing their belief in this world. How strongly you hold onto your belief will decide how successful you will become.

Chapter 10:

4 Ways to Deal with Feelings of Inferiority When Comparing to Others

When we're feeling inferior, it's usually a result of comparing ourselves to other people and feeling like we don't measure up. And let's be real, it happens all. The. Damn. Time. You could be scrolling through your Instagram feed, notice a new picture of someone you follow, and think: *Wow, how do they always look so perfect?! No amount of filters will make me look like that!* Or maybe you show up to a party, and you quickly realize you're in a room full of accomplished people with exciting lives, and the thought of introducing yourself sends you into a panic. Suddenly, you're glancing at the door and wondering what your best escape plan is. You could be meeting your partner's family for the first time, and you're worried that you won't fit in or that they'll think you're not good enough. You might feel easily intimidated by other people and constantly obsess over what they think of you, even though it's beyond your control.

Don't worry! We have some coping strategies for you that will help you work through your feelings. Try 'em out and see for yourself!

1. Engage in compassionate self-talk

When we feel inferior, we tend to pick ourselves apart and be hard on ourselves. Don't fall into the trap of being your own worst critic! Instead, build your <u>self-confidence</u> and self-esteem by saying positive things to yourself that resonate with you: *I'm feeling inferior right now, but I know my worth. I'm not defined by my credentials, my possessions, or my appearance. I am whole.*

2. Reach out for support or connect with a friend

Just like the Beatles song goes: *I get by with a little help from my friends!* Reach out to someone you can trust and who will be there for you. You might feel inferior now, but it doesn't mean you have to navigate it alone! Get all of those negative feelings off your chest. Having someone there to validate our feelings can be so helpful!

3. Give yourself a pep talk and utilize a helpful statement

Comparing ourselves to other people just brings down our mood and makes us feel like garbage. Sometimes, we gotta give ourselves a little pep talk to turn those negative thoughts around. *I feel inferior right now, but I can get through this! I'm not the only person who has felt this way, and I won't be the last. Everything is gonna be okay!*

4. Comfort yourself like a friend

If you don't have anyone who can be there for you at this moment, that's okay. You can be there for yourself! Think about how you would want a loved one to comfort you at this moment. Pat yourself on the back, treat yourself to some junk food, cuddle up on the couch with a warm, fuzzy blanket and binge your favorite show on Netflix. Be the friend you need right now!

PART 3

Chapter 1:

Constraints Make You Better: Why the Right Limitations Boost Performance

It is not uncommon to complain about the constraints in your life. Some people say that they have little time, money, and resources, or their network is limited. Yes, some of these things can hold us back, but there is a positive side to all of this. These constraints are what forces us to make choices and cultivate talents that can otherwise go undeveloped. Constraints are what drives creativity and foster skill development. In many ways reaching the next level of performance is simply a matter of choosing the right constraints.

How to Choose the Right Constraints

There are three primary steps that you can follow when you are using constraints to improve your skills.

1. Decide what specific skill you want to develop.

The more specific you are in the skill, the easier it will be to design a good constraint for yourself. You shouldn't try to develop the skill of being "good at marketing," for example. It's too broad. Instead, focus on learning how to write compelling headlines or analyze website data—something specific and tangible.

2. Design a constraint that requires this specific skill to be used

There are three main options for designing a constraint: time, resources, and environment.

- **Time:** Give yourself less time to accomplish a task or set a schedule that forces you to work on skills more consistently.

- **Resources:** Give yourself fewer resources (or different resources) to do a task.

- **Environment:** According to one study, if you eat on 10-inch plates rather than 12-inch plates, you'll consume 22 percent fewer calories over a year. One simple change in the environment can lead to significant results. In my opinion, environmental constraints are best because they impact your behavior without you realizing it.

3. Play the game

Constraints can accelerate skill development, but they aren't a magic pill. You still need to put in your time. The best plan is useless without repeated action. What matters most is getting your reps in.

The idea is to practice, experiment with different constraints to boost your skills. As for myself, I am working on storytelling skills these days. I have some friends who are amazing storytellers. I've never been great at it, but I'd like to get better. The constraint I've placed on myself is scheduling talks without the use of slides. My last five speaking engagements have used no slides or a few basic images. Without text to rely on, I have designed a constraint that forces me to tell better stories so that I don't embarrass myself in front of the audience.

So, the question here is What do you want to become great at? What skills do you want to develop? Most importantly, what constraints can you place upon yourself to get there? Figure these things out and start from today!

Chapter 2:

<u>10 Habits to Change Your Life</u>

I'm sure everyone wonders at a certain point in their life that what is the thing that is stopping them from reaching their goals. It is your bad and unhealthy habits that hold you down. If you want to succeed in life, you need to get rid of these habits and adopt healthy habits to help you in the long run.

Here are 10 healthy habits that will change your life completely if you can adopt them in your daily life:

1. Start Following a Morning Ritual

Everyone has something that they love to do, i.e., things that boost their energy and uplifts their mood. Find one for yourself and do that every morning. It will help you kickstart your day with a bright and cheerful mood. It will also help you to eliminate mental fatigue and stress. You will find yourself super energetic and productive. Let me tell you some morning rituals that you can try and get benefitted from.

- *Eating Healthy:* If you are very passionate about health and fitness, eating healthy as a morning ritual might be a win-win situation for you. You can have a nutritious breakfast every morning. Balance your breakfast with proper amounts of carbs, fats, proteins, etc. It will not only help you in staying healthy but will also help you kickstart your day on a proactive note.

- *Meditating:* Meditation is an excellent way of clearing your mind, enhancing your awareness, and improving your focus. You can meditate for 20 to 30 minutes every morning. Then you can take a nice warm shower, followed by a fresh cup of coffee. Most importantly, meditating regularly will also help you strengthen your immune system, promote emotional stability, and reduce stress.

- *Motivating:* A daily dose of motivation can work wonders for you. When you are motivated, your productivity doubles, and you make the best out of your day. Every morning, you can simply ask yourself questions like, "If it is the last day of your life, what do you want to do?", "What productive thing can I do today to make the best out of the day" "What do I need to do in order to avoid regretting later for having wasted a day?". When you ask yourself questions like these, you are actually instructing your brain to be prepared for having a packed-up and productive day.

- *Writing:* Writing can be a super-effective way of kickstarting your day. When you journal all your thoughts and emotions every day after waking up, it allows you to relieve yourself from all the mental clutter, unlocks your creative side, and sharpens your focus.

- *Working Out:* Working out is a great morning ritual that you can follow every day. When you work out daily, it helps you burn more fat, improves your blood circulation, and boosts your energy level. If you are interested in fitness and health, this is the perfect morning ritual for you. You can do some cardio exercises, or some strength training, or both. Depending on your suitability, create a workout routine for yourself and make sure to stick to that. If you don't stick to your routine, it won't be of much help.

•

2. Start Following the 80/20 Rule

The 80/20 rule states that almost 20% of the tasks you perform are responsible for yielding 80% of the results. It is why you should invest more time in tasks that can give you more significant results instead of wasting your time on tasks that yield little to no results. In this way, you can not only save time but also maximize your productivity. Most importantly, when you see the results after performing those tasks, you will be more motivated to complete the following tasks. After you have finished performing these tasks, now you can quickly move your concentration and focus towards other activities that you need to do throughout your day.

3. Practice Lots of Reading

Reading is a great habit and a great way to stimulate your creativity and gaining more knowledge. When you get immersed in reading, it calms you and improves your focus, almost similar to meditating. If you practice reading before going to bed, you are going to have a fantastic sleep. You can read non-fiction books, which will help you seek motivation, develop new ideas, and broaden your horizon. You can also get a lot of advice about how to handle certain situations in life.

4. Start Single-tasking

Multitasking is hard, and almost 2% of the world's total population can do this properly. You can try multitasking occasionally. If you keep on trying to do this all the time, it will form a mental clutter, and as a result, your brain won't be able to filter out unnecessary information. Many studies have suggested that it can severely damage your cognitive control and lower your efficiency when you multitask a lot. It is the main reason why you should try to do single-tasking more than multitasking. Prepare a list of all the tasks you need to perform in a day and start with the most important one. Make sure not to rush and to complete one thing at a time.

5. Start Appreciating More

Appreciating things is totally dependent on your mentality. For example, some people can whine and complain about a glass being half empty, whereas some people appreciate that there is half a glass of water. It totally depends on your point of view and way of thinking. People get blinded by the urge to reach success so much that they actually forget to appreciate the little things in life. If you are working and earning a handsome salary, don't just sit and complain about why you are not earning more, what you need to do to achieve that, etc. You should obviously aim high, but not at the cost of your well-being. When you practice gratitude, it increases your creativity, improves your physical health, and reduces your stress. You can start writing about the things you are grateful for in your journal every day before going to bed, make some time for appreciating your loved ones, or remind yourself of all the things you are grateful for before going to bed every day. If you are not happy with your current situation, you will not be happy in the future. You need to be happy and satisfied at first, and then only you can work on progressing further.

6. Always Keep Positive People Around You

When you have toxic people around you, it gets tough for you to stay in a good mood or achieve something good in life. Toxic people always find a way to pull you down and make you feel bad about yourself. You should always surround yourself with people who are encouraging and positive. When you do that, your life is going to be full of positivity.

7. Exercise on a Regular Basis

Start exercising regularly to maintain good health and enhancing your creativity and cognitive skills. It also increases your endurance level and boosts your energy. When you exercise regularly, your body produces more endorphins. These hormones work as anti-depressants.

8. Start Listening More

Effective communication is very important in maintaining both professional and personal relationships. For communicating effectively, you need to work on your listening capability first. You need to pay attention to the things said by others instead of focusing only on what you have to say. Listening to others will allow you to understand them better. When you listen to someone, it makes them understand that they are valued and that you are here to listen to them. When they feel important and valued, they also start paying attention to what you say, thereby contributing to effective communication. Don't try to show fake concentration while you are busy thinking about something else. When you listen more, you learn more.

9. Take a Break from Social Media (Social Media Detox)

Many studies have shown that excessive use of social media can contribute to depression. Most importantly, it wastes a lot of time because people meaninglessly scroll, swipe, and click for hours. It is a very unhealthy habit and is very bad for bothe physical and mental health. Sometimes you need to completely stop using social media for a while to reduce mental clutter and stress. Turn off your laptops and phones every day for a few hours. It will help you to reconnect with the surrounding world and will uplift your mood.

10. Start Investing More in Self-care

Make some time for yourself out of your busy schedule. It is going to boost your self-esteem, improve your mental health, and uplift your mood. You need to do at least one thing for yourself every day that will make you feel pampered and happy. You can prepare a mouth-watering meal, take a comfortable bubble bath, learn something new, or just relax while listening to music.

The moment you start introducing these habits in your daily, you will instantly see change. Remember that even a tiny step towards a positive change can give outstanding results if you stay consistent.

Chapter 3:

10 Habits of Warren Buffet

Warren Buffett, popularly known as the "Oracle of Omaha", is the chairman and CEO of Berkshire Hathaway and an American investor, corporate magnate, and philanthropist. He's undoubtedly a well-known investor of all time-if, not history, continuously setting records of knowledge, talent, and a strong drive to reach his future objectives. Buffett is also a supporter of leadership and personal growth, and he shares his wealth of advice to help you better your decisions.

So, how did he land to success? Here are ten warren's habits, which would you benefits later on.

1. His Reading Habit

Reading- a habit that he adheres to religiously, is one rule that Warren Buffett considers key to success. So he reads The Wall Street Journal, USA Today, and Forbes in the mornings and The Financial Times, The New York Times, Omaha World-Herald, and American Banker throughout the day.

Reading is basic to improving your understanding. Among other books, self-improvement books are popular with Buffet. That's said, consider jogging your memory with a mind-stimulating activity like reading. Engage in "500" pages book, article, newspaper each day, in the area that self-improves your interests. Reading makes you more knowledgeable than other people.

2. Compound Your Life and Finances

As per Albert Einstein, "Compound interest is the world's eighth wonder." if you understand it, you earn it; if not, you pay it." Warren Buffet's approach to investments never changes. He maintains his compounding investment principle as an investing strategy and aligns it with thinking patterns.

Compounding is the practice of reinvesting your earnings in your principal to generate an exponential return. Are you compounding your life finances, relationships, reading? That is how knowledge operates. It accumulates in the same way that compound interest does. You can accomplish it, but best when you're determined!

3. Isolation Power

Despite becoming the world's best investor and stock market trader, Warren Buffett claims that living away from Wall Street helped him. When you block the outside influence, you think quickly, distract unimportant variables and the general din.

Isolation exposes you to more prospects as it keeps you from external influence and information, making you unique and infamous.

4. Managing Your Time Wisely

You'll have 24 hours a day, or 1,440 minutes. All the leaders and successful people like Warren have one thing in common because of how powerful it is: Time management.

5. Do What You Enjoy

Your career or business may start with low returns but approaching it in Warren's way means switching your mind entirely to the job. If your mind likes something and you feed it to it regularly, it never turns off.

Working for a low salary is a momentary inconvenience, but it multiplies at the rate your skills increases, and they grow tremendously because you enjoy doing it.

6. Inner and Outer Scorecards

The key question about how people act is whether they have an Internal or an outward scorecard. So, naturally, it is preferable to be happy with your Inner Score to live a peaceful and happy life.

Having an inner scorecard is being contented with your thoughts and making decisions based on those thoughts while ignoring external influences or judgement skills. The deal is to live through values that matter to you, especially when making tough financial decisions.

7. Mimic the Finest Managers' Leadership Behaviours

Much of your life endeavours are, in most cases, shaped by the person who you choose to admire and emulate. Warren's admiration of Tom Murphy scourged him to greatness in leading his businesses to success.

8. Understand What You Have

Know and understand the companies in which you have a stake. Examine and analyze what is going on within the company, not what is going on in the marketplace.

The company's operations should be straightforward such that you can explain to an 8-year-old child how the company produces money in one phase. Familiarize enough with your investments while keeping a tab with its exact worth.

9. Invest in Your Well-Being

The basic right towards success is your well-being. Take care of your mental and physical health first, especially when you're young. The importance of life's fundamentals- nutritious diet, regular exercise, and restful sleep-is self-evident. It all boils down to whether you're doing them correctly.

10. Create a Positive Reputation

Buffett's reputation stems from his moral and level-headed attitude to both his personal and business life. You should view your business/career as a reflection of yourself, which means you should be careful and sensitive of how your decisions influence others.

Conclusion

Just as Warren, enhance your cognitive skills through learning to become more knowledgeable for bettering your life initiatives. While focusing on your major goals, take care of your mental and physical well-being.

Therefore, invest your efforts and time carefully because the returns will multiply eventually.

Chapter 4:

10 Habits of Elon Musk

An alternator, Inventor, and a Disruptor! These phrases and Elon Musk are very synonymous. As a founder of such platforms as PayPal, Tesla, and SpaceX, Musk is worth being associated with these words! Every time Musk sits in his office means surprising the world with a new Corvette, as he did recently, by launching the 50th SpaceX. Whether you want to be an inventive business person or an employee, you can learn a lot from this authentic Iron Man.

These ten habits will uncover how Musk achieved his dreams, and so can you.

1. Before life gets in your way, take risks.

The perfect time to be an entrepreneur is when you are young. Responsibilities grow as you get older. Musk always encourages young people to take risks by doing something daring. Because as one gets old, responsibilities pile up.

Risk-taking has an impact on your family and children as you become older. Not to mention that you'll have less free time. Instead, take chances now when you don't have any other obligations or time constraints.

2. To Lead, Read

Formal education may come to an end, but your street smartness shouldn't. As Musk said, "You have no idea things you don't know that are out there." This is entirely true. Musk read the entire *Britannica Encyclopedia* as a child while most of us were reading the *Goodnight Moon*. His reading habit has only accelerated as he has gotten older. Are you able to claim the same position about your reading patterns?

Immerse yourself in the literature that will broaden your scope and provide you with new ideas and perspectives. It should come as no surprise that the best learners are also the best earners in society.

3. Ignite the Midnight Energy.

As dedicated as he is to his work, Musk's work ethic is notoriously perfect. He works for up to a hundred hours across his many businesses. You don't have to do the same, but keep Elon in mind the next time you're fatigued or when you aren't motivated. He is an example of what pushing yourself looks like. If you do not follow suit, you may be squandering your potential.

4. Make a Plan for Success, but Be Prepared To Fail.

There is no such thing as a successful crystal ball. Even Musk had no idea how his Tesla Motors would fare. However, as he put it, "When something is valuable enough, you can try even though failure is the likely outcome." It would help if you made every effort to have your dreams come true. But also be prepared for anything just in case things don't work out as planned. With a backup plan in place, it is easier to overcome the failures.

5. Complaining Is a Game-Changer.

The majority of individuals grumble about traffic. Elon Musk is not one of them. Rather than complaining about the situation, Musk sought a remedy. This gave rise to an actual Company, which aims to reduce traffic congestion by building a subway system. Creating a future for yourself is the most effective strategy to attain the outcomes you desire. This was a lesson that enabled Kogan of Wolfie to grow his business. "Complaints are an indication that there is a problem that needs to be solved," he explains. "Listening to grievances is a fantastic method to come up with fresh ideas that people genuinely need."

6. Be Yourself.

"Don't just go with the flow," Musk advised. Most of the notable thriving businesses concentrate on developing breakthroughs. They do not attempt to outrun the opponent. Affirming this notion is the CEO and founder of the Viral Content Marketing-Jonny Videl. "Going viral isn't something that happens by chance," he explains. "Instead of pursuing others, stand firmly by putting your focus on whatever makes you unique.

7. Competing With Anyone Else Makes You Bitter.

In life, there is always a second chance for improvement. As Musk noted, it's critical to have a feedback mechanism in place, where you're constantly contemplating what you have achieved and how to do it better. That, I believe, is the most crucial nugget of advice: embrace continuous questioning of every detail of what you have done and consider ways of doing things better. Don't be afraid of unfavorable feedback because it frequently uncovers new ideas.

8. Treat Your Stakeholders As if They Were Family

Treat your co-workers or your customers as they were your own. Musk, for example, is always thanking and appreciating his customers on Twitter daily. People will always notice modest gestures, no matter how small they are. Most successful people like Maulik Parekh-President and CEO of SPi CRM, have emulated this habit, and it seems to be working. Speaking to an interview, Maulik noted, "Our personnel is our most valuable asset. If we look after them, they will look after the business. What we do for our employees is what we do for your clients." Take time outside your corner office to develop the foundations of your firm through employee and customer interactions.

9. Spending All of Your Money on Advertising Is Not a Good Idea.

Musk does not squander money on advertising. Instead, he asks, "Will this activity result in a better product or service?" This one pain to hear as a marketer. But try to understand Musk's reasoning. A high-quality product will generate a lot of positive word of mouth. Concentrate on that first, and the rest will fall into place.

10.See the Best in Everything That You Do.

To do good, you don't have to transform the world entirely. However, you should constantly strive to deliver genuine value. According to Musk, producing something of great importance, however little it is, if it achieves the modest bit of good for a huge crowd, then it's acceptable. Things don't have to transform the world to be perfect. See the positivity in every detail of your work. No matter how small it is, it will motivate you.

Conclusion

Whatever your life goals are, emulating Elon Musk's habits and way of thinking can help you get there. The extra work you put into reaching your life goals will have a significant impact on your future.

Chapter 5:

Seven Habits That Will Make You Successful

A man's habits are as good as his lifestyle. Some habits are akin to successful people. The path to greatness is less traveled and the habits to success may be difficult for some people to sustain.

The road to success is narrow and occasionally thorny because habits that will make you successful are uncomfortable and difficult to adapt. Similar to Charles Darwin's theory of survival for the fittest, only those who manage to trim their excesses and shape their habits will eventually be successful.

Here are seven habits that will make you successful:

1. Integrity

Integrity is one of the measures of success. It is the ability to live an honest life free from swindling, blackmail, and corruption among other vices. Integrity is the morality of a person and is relative from one person to another. However, there is a generally accepted threshold of integrity expected of people in different social, political, and economic classes.

Integrity is uncommon to most people making it highly valuable. People will forget how you looked but will never forget how you made them feel. Integrity holds back one from committing such awful mistakes. It will help you award the deserving, condemn vices, be intolerable to corruption, and make transparency your middle name.

The lack of integrity is responsible for the downfall of great people and business empires. Political leaders worldwide have lost their crown of glory to corruption. They were once the dream of every pupil in school and aspiring young leaders looked up to them. Corruption and greed stole that from them.

So powerful is integrity that successful people guard theirs' tooth and nail. Once eroded, their success is at stake. It may crumble down like a mound hill. Do you want to be successful? Have integrity.

2. An Open Mind

It is the ability to tolerate and be receptive to divergent ideas different from your beliefs. It takes a lot to accommodate the opinions of others and accept their reasoning to be rational. Successful people fully understand that they do not have a monopoly on brilliant ideas. As such, they cautiously welcome the proposals of other people while allowing room for further advancement.

Entertaining the ideas of other people does not mean blindly accepting them. It is the habit of successful people to be critical of everything, balancing their options and only settling for the best. An open mind translates to an analytical and inquisitive nature. The zeal to venture into the unknown and experiment with new waters.

Successful people are distinguished from others because they challenge the status quo. They seek to improve their best and develop alternatives to the existing routines. The reason why they are successful in the first place is their open mind.

How does one have an open mind? It is by being open to infinite possibilities of a hundred and one ways of approaching issues. Routine is an enemy of open-mindedness and by extension, success. It is of course inevitable not to follow a routine at our places of work, schools, or families. It is acceptable to that extent. Being its slave is completely unacceptable.

3. Move With Time

Time is never stagnant. The world evolves around time and seasons. The wise is he who deciphers and interprets them correctly. The measure of success in these modern times is different from those in the ancient days. A lot has changed.

In this era of technological advancements, we cannot afford to live in analog ways. The poor readers of seasons are stagnant in one position for a long time. Success is elusive in their hands. A look at business giants will reveal their mastery of times and seasons. They do not fumble at it. Not one bit.

Successful businesses deal with tools of the trade of the modern world. From the great Microsoft corporation to the Coca-cola company. All of them align themselves with the market demand presently. Learning the present time and season is a habit that will elevate you to success.

4. Learn From The Mistakes of Others

It is prudent to learn from the mistakes of other people and not from yours. Keenly observe those ahead of you and watch out not to fall into their traps. It is regretful to be unable to take a cue from our predecessors and learn from their failures.

Successful people travel down roads once taken (for the advantage of hindsight) by others – except for a few adventurous ones who venture into the unknown. The benefit of hindsight is very important because we learn from the mistakes of those who preceded us and adjust accordingly. Develop a habit of watching closely those ahead of you and take a cue from them not to commit similar mistakes. This habit will propel you to the doorstep of success.

5.   Investment Culture

It is prudent to be mindful of tomorrow. No amount of investment is too little. Successful people do not consume everything they produce. They save a portion of their income for the future. Investment is a culture developed over time. Some people find it difficult to postpone the entire consumption of their income. They will only settle when nothing is left. This is retrogressive.

An investment culture curbs wastage and emphasizes tomorrow's welfare. Moreover, to reduce risk, the investment portfolio is diversified. It is dangerous to risk everything in one endeavor. Captains of industries worldwide have invested broadly in different sectors. This makes them stay afloat even during tough economic seasons.

6.   Choosing Your Battles

On your way to success, do not make many enemies. This habit is ancient but very relevant to date. Unnecessary fights will wear you out and divert you away from the goal. Petty distractions will hijack your focus and successfully make you unsuccessful.

Learn to train your guns on things that matter. Feed your focus and starve your fears. Ignore useless petty issues that may lead to tainting of your public image. Fight your battles wisely.

7. Learn To Listen

Listening is an art beyond hearing. It is paying detailed attention to the speech of others, both verbal and non-verbal. Always listen more and talk less – a common argument for having two ears and one mouth. To be successful, you will have to pay closer attention to what is unspoken. Listen to the way people communicate. You will pick up genuine intentions in their speech and align yourself accordingly.

Once perfected, these seven habits will make you successful.

Chapter 6:

7 Habits That Are Good For You

The cognitive ability to distinguish what is good from what is bad for us is an invaluable skill. Cherry-picking nutritive habits in a world full of all manner of indecency comes handy especially if you want to stand out from the crowd.

Here are 7 habits that are good for you:

1. Waking Up Early

The early bird catches the worm. Early risers have the opportunity to pick the best for themselves before the rest of the world is awake. It is healthy and prudent to wake up early and start your day before most people do. You leverage on opening your business early before your competitors. Besides, the preparedness of early risers is unmatched even as the day progresses.

Waking up early is not a reserve for 'busy people' only. It is for everyone in this world of survival for the fittest. We all have 24 hours in one day. The difference comes from how we use our time. One may spend more than 8 hours sleeping and another will spend just 6 hours for the same. You cannot sleep as if you are competing with the dead and expect to make it in the land of the living.

Early risers are active people. They are as alert as chamois, prepared for any eventuality.

2. Associate With Successful People

Show me your friends and I will show you what kind of person you are. Success, like most things, is contagious. In his book *48 laws of power*, Robert Greene writes *'avoid the unhappy and unlucky.'* This is not discrimination. Association with the unhappy and unlucky will contaminate you with negative energy.

Associate with successful people and you will follow their example. You will emulate their saving culture, their investment behavior, and their aggressiveness in business. In the shadow of the successful, you will attract positivity and grow exponentially. Maintain knit relationships with the successful.

3. Be Teachable

A teachable spirit will take you places where your character will not. A teachable person is capable of receiving correction graciously without perceiving it as demeaning. Do not be afraid of getting things wrong. Instead, be worried when you lack the humility to accept correction.

Being teachable is one of the greatest strengths you can have. We all are a work in progress, never finished products. What happens when you refuse to be under the tutelage of the successful and experienced? The greatest lessons are not learned in a classroom but the school of life.

4. Accepting Challenges

When challenged by circumstances we face, be the bigger brother/sister. Take challenges positively and work towards a solution instead of whining about this or that. Our patience, skills, and competence are sometimes put to the test. A test so subtle that we fail without even realizing it. When you have a positive mindset of accepting challenges, you will ace the game. Prove your worth wherever you are through your actions, never by your words.

When you accept a challenge and conquer it, it takes you to another level. The beauty of life lies in progress with the assurance that change is a constant. Accept challenges towards positivity and not the dark ones. Ignore that which derails your purpose or goes against your principles.

5. Learn When To Retreat and To Advance

The art of knowing when to push or pull is important in life. On the battlefield, retreating and advancing by troops is a call their leader makes. He decides that for his team based on his training, the immediate situation, and his judgment. Retreating is not a sign of weakness; neither is advancing a sign of strength. Both are strategies to win a war.

It is okay to retreat from a cause you were pursuing or to adjust your plans. Just make it worth your while. When you resume, be stronger than before. Again, when you retreat, do not succumb to the ridicule of your enemies when they mistake it for weakness. The fear of what the opinion of others (non-entities) is should not make you afraid of retreating to strategize.

When you make up your mind to advance with a noble course, advance skillfully. Do not advance blindly or ignorant of what you intend to achieve. Train your focus on the target.

6. Ask for help.

We are mortals; facing deficiencies here and there. We do not always have the answer to everything. Ask for help from the knowledgeable ones when in a quagmire.

Asking for help is not a weakness. It is appreciating the strengths of others. It is also appreciating the diversity of the human race that we are not endowed with everything. The silent rule is that you should be careful whom you approach for help. Some ill-intentioned people will sink you deep into trouble.

Nevertheless, asking for help is perfectly normal and it is something you should try sometimes. When you ask for help from the experienced, you save yourself the trouble of making messy mistakes. Learn through others who trod down the same road. Their lessons are invaluable; you will avoid their mistakes.

7. <u>Develop hobbies.</u>

Hobbies are those things you engage in for fun. They are very important because you take a break from your daily hustles. In your hobbies, you are carefree. You do not have to worry about your boss or business partners.

Hobbies are meant to be fun. If you are not having fun when doing your hobbies, probably they are no longer one. You should consider finding new ones. All work without play makes Jack a dull boy.

Hobbies are good for you. Go for swimming or that road trip, find a sport and play for fun, go beyond singing in the shower, travel everywhere you desire, or even start watching that TV series you are always curious about. Variety is the spice of life. Do not be afraid to spice up your life with all that your heart desires.

The above 7 habits are good for you. They will help you grow and increase your productivity in all you do.

Chapter 7:

6 Ways To Get Full Attention From People Around You

The long-term success of someone's life depends on getting the attention of others. Those others can include your teammates, your boss, your life partner, your clients, etc. But how? A person may ask. You cannot get promoted without getting your boss's attention, and your work cannot get appreciated by your teammates without awareness. To lead a healthy personal life, one may need to give attention to and from one's life partner, and of course, without the attention of your clients, how will your business survive?

Fortunately, there is plenty of research on how a human brain works and how it can focus on something. A lot of people have been researching about gaining people's attention for a long time now.

By some researchers, attention has been considered the "most important currency anybody can give you," although attention does make a person feel loved, it also gains your success. Fame can even come through negative attention, but it comes with hate as its price, whereas true and long-term success comes from positive attention. Here are six ways to get full attention from people around you.

1. Stand In A Central Position

When you are at a social gathering or a party, place yourself in a central position. Try to appear more friendly to new people, invite them over to your group, this way people will like you more. When you speak, they will pay attention—standing in a prominent place where everybody can see and talk to you easily will gain you more alert. Be being friendly to new individuals, and you will feel connected to others. Just be confident the whole time, and try to blend well with others and stand in a prominent place; this way, you will get more attention.

2. Leave Some Mystery!

Do you know what Zeigarnik Effect is? This effect suggests that the human brain tends to remember those things more, which is incomplete, as the question in their brain arises how? Where? And what?

This kind of technique is often used by professionals in business meetings, audience-oriented presentations. However, you can also use it in your daily life. When you introduce yourself to someone, don't just spill everything about yourself right away. Give the tiniest bit of pieces of information about something interesting, don't give the details just yet;

wait for someone to ask for the details. And someone will surely ask, and you will get the desired attention.

3. Use Body Language

Most of us know how to communicate verbally, but do you know how to communicate non-verbally? Because non-verbal communication is as important as verbal communication. Maintain positive body language, and if you sit back slouched and give some closed-off vibes, it is less likely that you would catch someone's attention. To see some attention, you need to bring more positivity in your conversation and your body language. Don't cross your arms and legs when talking to someone; face them with an open posture and stand with confidence. Don't avoid eye contact but don't overdo it; try to maintain eye contact with everyone around you for a while. This will show your confidence and also builds a connection with others. Be relaxed confidently. Smiling while talking to someone indicates your friendliness and makes them feel welcome; this way, they feel comfortable and give you their undivided attention, but everybody would avoid talking to you if you look moody.

4. Leave An Impression

It is the subconscious habit of a human being to think more about the people who left a good impression on them, try to engage their senses like touch, hear, or vision. Who doesn't like fashion nowadays? Try to wear something fashionable and decent, the kind of outfit that will likely leave a good impression on others. You can also wear something that has a different color or a twist to it. Speak confidently and in a clear voice. You can also put on a lovely perfume, cologne; try not to go overboard with this as nobody likes too much smell even if it is good.

5. Having A Hype Team

Having a hype team can easily capture a lot of attention; when you are in a not so formal setting, bring along your friends, surely they will be more than happy to excite you up. When you talk about your achievements among other people, it may seem to some that you are simply bragging. Still, when someone else talks about your accomplishments, it increases the interest of other people in you and gains you some positive attention.

6. Find A Way To Sell Yourself Without Bragging

A hype team is not always an option, but selling yourself without bragging is also something that needs to be done. What you don't need to discuss is;

- Your bank balance
- The expensive things you own
- Your occupation
- Your achievement

Conclusion

Brag through storytelling, and everybody loves an inspiring story. A successful person with a humble background always gains some attention. Attention plays an essential role in our lives, and you need to put a bit of effort into gaining it.

CPSIA information can be obtained
at www.ICGtesting.com
Printed in the USA
BVHW041445071221
623422BV00015B/1060